ARE YOU still KIDDING ME?

STACEY GUSTAFSON

LUMINARE PRESS
WWW.LUMINAREPRESS.COM

Although a few names have been changed, this is a work of nonfiction and any resemblance to real people and events is probably true.

Are You Still Kidding Me? (Keep Kidding Me Series – Book 2)
© 2018 Stacey Gustafson

All rights reserved. This book or any portion thereof may not be reproduced or used in any manner whatsoever without the express written permission of the publisher, except for the use of brief quotations in a book review.

Printed in the United States of America

Cover Design: Claire Flint Last
Cover Photograph of the Author: Suzan Petersen Artistic Photography

Luminare Press
438 Charnelton St., Suite 101
Eugene, OR 97401
www.luminarepress.com

LCCN: 2018945250
ISBN: 978-1-944733-60-5

To Mom and Dad

Thanks for teaching me that anything can be accomplished with hard work and dedication.

To Mike, Ashley, and Brock

Laughter has bonded our family together. Thanks for feeling the freedom to share your thoughts, ideas, and dreams with me.

> I consider myself a survivor of the outdoor playground equipment, cars without seatbelts, and secondhand smoke.
>
> —Stacey Gustafson, *Stand-Up Comedy Night*, Erma Bombeck Writers' Workshop, Dayton, Ohio

OTHER NONFICTION BY STACEY GUSTAFSON

~~~~~~

Are You Kidding Me?
My Life With an Extremely Loud Family,
Bathroom Calamities, and Crazy Relatives

#1 Amazon Best Seller in Parenting & Family Humor and Motherhood

~~~~~~

"Gustafson covers much the same ground as Erma Bombeck, but updated for the 21st century, with a splash of Seinfeld-esque observational humor mixed in… Gustafson can be grouchy, but she's never mean-spirited, and while she complains freely about her hubby and kids, she's clearly, at heart, a loving wife and mom."

—ROZ WARREN,
Huffington Post

PRAISE FOR *ARE YOU STILL KIDDING ME?*

"I love Stacey Gustafson's voice—her stories and how she shares them! She is entertaining, relevant and relatable, and her new book is for anyone who is a parent, child, spouse, or other."

—Wendy Liebman, stand-up comedian, semi-finalist on *America's Got Talent, Season 9, Taller on TV.*

"Stacey Gustafson is like the sister you always wanted in the suburbs: Funny, just a little bit snarky, and the perfect partner in crime against kids, husbands, and uptight fashionista moms. Her new book finds the humor in all those outrageous parenting moments that threaten your sanity in a way that is completely relatable and totally hysterical."

—Tracy Beckerman, syndicated columnist and author of *Lost in Suburbia, a Momoir*

"Stacey's next set of adventures are as humorous as her first. Even though her kids are now grownups the family funny has not ended."

—Joel Madison, actor, television comedy writer and producer for *Roseanne, The Fresh Prince of Bel-Air,* and HBO's *Crashing*

"I'm grateful life continues to kid Stacey Gustafson so she can write hilarious and relatable anecdotes about family, marriage, midlife, and other mysteries. A true humorist, she leaves readers laughing and never goes past her allotted time."

—Elaine Ambrose, syndicated blogger and author of 10 books, including *Menopause Sucks and Midlife Cabernet*

"I love that Stacey Gustafson is "still kidding me"—her stories are my LOL therapy. "I Netflix Cheated on my Husband" is worth the price of admission as is "Redecorating Do Us Part." When life bears down on me a little too hard, I reach for *Are You Still Kidding Me?* and my soul is bathed in tears of laughter."

—Suzette Martinez Standring, award-winning author, syndicated columnist, speaker, and TV show host

"Step into the funny and spot-on details of Stacey's life in all of its comedic chaos. Her relatable stories cover everything from babies to bingo to binge-watching faux pas and all stops in between. You'll find yourself laughing with each new story because it has either happened to you or you're so glad it has NOT happened to you. A fun quick-witted read."

—Regina Stoops, comedian, blogger, *Normal Notes* at reginastoops.com

"Stacey Gustafson's hilarious new book, *Are You Still Kidding Me?*, is like getting together with your best friends to laugh, cry, and laugh some more. Stacey brings the funny in everyday situations to life. You'll want to get several copies of *Are You Still Kidding Me?* to share its wonderfully relatable humor with your sisters and friends. A great gift for every woman in your life, including you!"

—Gina Valley, editor, blogger at *The Glamorous Life Of The Modern Day Soccer Mom*

CONTENTS

OTHER NONFICTION BY STACEY GUSTAFSON VI
PRAISE FOR *ARE YOU STILL KIDDING ME?* XI
HELLO, IT'S STILL ME, STACEY 1

KIDS

DOG DAYS OF MOVING 7
OPERATION SPLASHDOWN 12
GETTING TO KNOW MY SON ONE TOE AT A TIME 16
ONE-UPPED BY EXPERTS 20
GROWING UP IN THE LAUNDRY ROOM 25
SMOKIN' HOT SUMMER VACATION 29
MAMA'S HUNGRY 33
HELICOPTER MOM 36
TO CATCH A THIEF 41
I NEED MORE BANDWIDTH 44
YOUNG ENTREPRENEUR 49
YOU ARE MY FAVORITE 53

HUSBANDS

I NETFLIX CHEATED ON MY HUSBAND 59
REDECORATING DO US PART 63
WHEN CHURCH PEOPLE KNOCK 67
GRAND THEFT AUTO 70

ROCK-A-BYE BABY	74
MIKE SAVES EUROPE	77
ASLEEP AT THE WHEEL	81
TWO THUMBS UP	85
MONEY TALKS	90
HOTLIPS HOULIHAN AND THE NEEDY PATIENT	94
BRAIN FARTS	98
SHAKE YOUR BOOTY	102

PARENTS

BINGO AIN'T FOR SISSIES	109
ALEXA, TURN ON THE OVEN	113
ONE WOMAN MEDICAL DISPENSARY	117
CLUELESS IN PARIS	120
NEAR CHRISTMAS BIRTHDAY BLUES	126
BLUE APRON STRESS	130
THE HUNDRED-FOOT JOURNEY	133
DOWNSIZING CHRISTMAS	137
WORLD'S BEST DAUGHTER	141

OTHERS

FOR A GOOD TIME, CALL	147
GALLBLADDER MATTERS	151
SHAKE, RATTLE, AND ROLL	156
I ATTRACT WEIRDOS	159
I SPY WITH MY LITTLE EYE	163

SOMEWHAT IRRATIONAL FEARS	167
POTTERY BARN DEBACLE	170
SHENANIGANS	173
KEEP YOUR HANDS TO YOURSELF	177
WAYS TO DIE IN CANADA	181
MICK JAGGER KEEPS ME UP AT NIGHT	185
YOU'LL THANK ME LATER	188
ACKNOWLEDGEMENTS	193
ABOUT STACEY	195

HELLO, IT'S STILL ME, STACEY...

Let me start by properly introducing myself. I'm Stacey Gustafson, married with two children. Since the release of my last book, *Are You Kidding Me? My Life with an Extremely Loud Family, Bathroom Calamities, and Crazy Relatives*, I'm proud to call myself an author, blogger, and stand-up comedian. You may ask, "How'd that happen?" Well, grab a chair.

After twenty some-odd years, my kids left home. Kapow! They're out of here, and now I'm an empty nester. Remember when you thought fights and complaints about dinner would never end? Or what about the broken promises to do the laundry, clean the kitchen, feed the dog, and others. No more. Now it's just my husband and me. We fight over the remote control and whose turn it is to get the mail. Minor stuff.

My work as a mom appears complete. Well, maybe not 100%. Surely, there will be the occasional phone call from my kids, questions asked about the best way to fold a fitted sheet, write a check, roast a chicken, drive a stick-shift, and read cursive. But for the most part, our daughter and son are out of the nest.

For two decades, I was the glitter picker-upper, carpool driver, bug killer, lunch lady, homework finder, boo-boo kisser, listener, hugger, and family cheerleader. It was a good run. Not one serial killer in the bunch.

As a family, fun still rules at Sunday dinners, spontaneous get-togethers, and our yearly vacations. We goof around by rattling off funny lines from movies like *School of Rock* to make each other laugh, but things have changed. I'm glad I remembered to take notes. Our kids are more independent, with one off the payroll entirely. It was time to explore my own interests.

I started a bucket list; stuff I wanted to do after my kids were grown and flown. On it were the usual things; travel, eat better, do yoga, nap, read more, and volunteer, but number one has always been to do stand-up comedy. I've never shared this with anyone because I believed that would jinx it.

I've always loved everything about comedy; from hilarious sitcoms like *Black-ish* and *Modern Family* to guaranteed-to-make-you-laugh authors like Nora Ephron and Dave Barry. But what I enjoy the most is stand-up comedy. I've always admired that guy or gal who could stand up in front of a crowd and tell jokes, hecklers be damned!

Twenty-five years ago, I imagined myself on stage doing the opening act for one of my favorites, Tim Allen. We saw him perform in Atlanta before he appeared on the TV series, *Home Improvement*, and I wondered, "What's it feel like to have the full attention of an audience?"

As a young, married couple, when our favorite comedians like Kathleen Madigan, Jim Gaffigan, Brian Regan, and Sinbad were in town, my husband and I found a way to scrape together enough money for tickets.

Fast-forward to today.

Since I published my first book, I've received speaking engagments and been paid for a few of them. Yet the thought of speaking in front of a group made me as nervous as a pig at a barbeque. Until now, the mighty pen was my mouthpiece. I expressed myself through my blog, Facebook, and humorous short stories. Face-to-face contact, not for me.

Then everything changed. I joined a public speaking club to feel more comfortable in front of an audience and polish my speaking skills. Then I decided to push myself even further.

I caught the stand-up bug at a writers' conference four years ago. The featured comedian convinced me to do my four-minute set on mammograms to an audience of over 350 supportive and hilarious writers. Their claps and cheers invigorated me. I wanted to try it again.

At home, I polished my skills and practiced, practiced, practiced. I searched for my comedic voice and decided on storytelling, using material from my book.

I found a local comedy club that held Open Mic Night. Thirty comics debuted and only three were women. And then it happened. I won Best Comic of the Month at Open Mic Night with the help of over seventy friends and family in the audience. The club ran out of food, making up for it with free margaritas. My biggest compliment of the night? My daughter said, "Congratulations, you broke Tommy T's."

Afterward, a local comedian asked me to make a special guest appearance at a community fundraiser. Sharing my comedy on stage to raise money for worthy causes, like local schools, cancer, and performing arts, consumes me. Stand-up gives me purpose.

I've even met Wendy Liebman, semi-finalist from *America's Got Talent, Season 9*. She told me after my turn at stand-up in Dayton, Ohio, "You're a natural." That's a mighty high compliment I'll never forget!

Needless to say, my life has changed since I published my first book four years ago. I'm thrilled you decided to check it out, the one you're holding, *Are You Still Kidding Me?* It's chock full of short stories meant to elicit snorting, because I'm guessing you'll see yourself in many of them.

Have you ever been tempted to change your kid's essay? Do you consider blocking your child's return home from college because they hog your bandwidth? Ever Netflix cheat on your husband? Try to explain Alexa to your mother? I've been told you'll find my stories relatable, another day in the life of an average suburban family.

For me, writing has been my way of expression and stand-up is a new opportunity to push myself further and share humor with others. The way I see it, we can sit in a rocking chair waiting for grandkids or embrace change and take a chance. Who knows, you might surprise yourself. I did.

KIDS

"I've made questionable parenting decisions."

—Stacey Gustafson, *One Night, Three Women, Too Funny*, Bothwell Arts Center, Livermore, California

DOG DAYS OF MOVING

All I needed to know about moving I learned from having a baby: there will be crying, shit happens, and you will swear never to do it again.

After my husband and I moved for the fourth time in five years of marriage, I could pack up a house before he came home for dinner. Box up kitchen supplies, check. Bubble wrap fragile items, no problem. Shut down utilities, piece of cake. But this time we had added a fourteen-pound hitch to our smooth plans—our three-month-old baby girl who presented a new set of issues. What will I do when my baby needs a nap? Where will I breastfeed? How can I stay out of the movers' way? I needed an escape plan for the next twelve hours.

"It's settled," said Mike, plopping down in the nearest recliner. "I'll organize the move at the old house, and you stay at Jim and Mary's new home." Our friends lived nearby, no kids. They'd be at work, and I could hang out at their place.

On packing day, a team of burly men wearing weight-lifting belts tackled our belongings in a flurry of plastic wrap, packing paper, and clear tape. This was my cue to dodge the chaos. Armed with extra diapers, wet wipes, car seat, bouncy seat, blankets, and baby toys, I held Ashley over my shoulder and banged on Jim and Mary's front door at 6:00 AM.

"Gosh, thanks for letting us stay here," I said, rocking to and fro. "Our house is a mess."

"Glad to help," he said giving me the thumbs up. "Mary usually works from home but today she's out of town. Do you mind letting Max out later?" Max, their golden retriever, danced around at the mention of his name.

"Got it," I said with a smile. "See you after work."

I spread a soft blanket on the living room floor and set up the rest of the baby gear. I sang to Ashley as I carried her around and pointed out all the new sights, like fresh flowers on the end table and a fuzzy dog toy. She jumped whenever Max barked.

"It's okay," I said to Ashley. "He's friendly." The dog licked her tiny arms with his wet tongue.

After I breastfed Ashley, she rubbed her eyes with her pudgy fist which signaled naptime. I put her into the car seat on the coffee table, grabbed *People Magazine* and snuggled on the sofa.

Max tap-danced near the back door, toenails clicking on the tile floor.

I'm coming. I'm coming.

Max bolted outside and scrambled behind a tree. I snooped around their backyard. *Nice abode.* Jim must be doing well at his sales job.

Max finished his business and scratched at the screen door to get back in. I turned the doorknob and…locked? I twisted the knob faster than a DJ at a rave party. It wouldn't budge.

My mind whirled with a million bad things that

could happen in the next few minutes. My baby might crash down off the coffee table. A fire could suddenly ignite and engulf the house in flames. A kidnapper could swoop in and snatch my baby. My chest heaved. My heart raced.

What if she chokes and I can't help her?

I dashed to the front of the house and cut my legs on the rose bushes in my way. I spied my precious bundle through the window, tucked in a car seat smack dab asleep in the center of the coffee table.

I'm going to kill Mike. This is all his fault. I never wanted to move in the first place.

Back in the day, cell phones were only used by corporate hotshots, not stay-at-home moms. I banged on the neighbor's door.

"I locked my baby in Jim's house and can't get back in," I screeched, twisting my wedding ring. "Can I use your phone?"

"Oh, dear," the neighbor lady said, waving me into the kitchen.

First, I called Mike. "Help," I whined. "Jim's back door automatically locked behind me. Ashley's trapped inside."

"I can't leave. Stuck here with the movers," he said raising his voice. "Call Jim. He's got the key."

A meltdown brewed deep in my gut. My eyes twitched and my arms flushed a deep crimson.

Did this man not understand what I was saying? Call the police or SWAT team for God's sake. Do something.

"DID-YOU-HEAR–ME-COR-RECT-LY?" I said. "ASH-LEY'S-LOCKED-IN-SIDE-THE-HOUSE-IN-A-CAR-SEAT-YOU-IDIOT. GET-HERE-NOW."

"She'll be okay for a few minutes," he said with a sigh. "Just call Jim."

"You're such a jerk. You only care about yourself. I can't believe we're moving again."

I slammed down the phone and called Jim. "Ashley's locked inside your house. I need you to come home now."

"Uh…I can leave in about an hour and a half."

"If you're not here in fifteen minutes, I'm breaking down the door," I shouted.

"I'm leaving," he said.

Yeah, you better be!

I slapped down the receiver and darted around the house to check for open windows or unlocked doors. Their place was sealed as tight as the packaging on a stack of baseball cards.

Then someone tapped my shoulder.

"Need help?" asked a lanky, dark-haired older guy. "I live next-door."

"I'm so happy to see you," I said with shaky hands. "I'm staying at Jim and Mary's. Can't get back in the damn door. My baby's inside."

He used a screwdriver to force the sliding glass door off its rails. Like a genie, he lifted the glass door and poof, we were inside.

I snatched up Ashley and held her tight. She cried out in surprise.

"Thanks so much," I said to the neighbor with a big hug. "I was freaking out. You're my savior."

Out front, two cars screeched to a halt. I rushed outside with Ashley in my arms, Max following close behind.

"Honey, are you okay?" my husband said then planted a smooch. "I'm so sorry."

"God, I'm glad to see you. I can't wait until we get to our new place. I love you."

"Thanks for helping," Jim said to his neighbor, shaking his hand. "I left work as fast as I could."

"It turned out fine," I said. "Hey, there goes Max."

Max raced down the street and rounded the corner at the end of the road. Jim took off for the chase.

"See you in an hour and a half," I yelled after Jim as Mike and I strolled to the car.

Run, Max, run!

OPERATION SPLASHDOWN

My four-year-old daughter, Ashley, displayed unbridled enthusiasm for playtime. A promise of a day at the zoo resulted in earth-shattering squeals as she ran around the kitchen island and screamed, "I love you, Mommy. Let's go. Let's go." A trip to the ice cream store caused her to burst into a Disney song.

"Zip-a-dee-doo-dah, Zip-a-dee-ay! My, oh my, what a wonderful day!"

When you raise an extrovert, it's mandatory to release her exuberance with outdoor playtime. Twice weekly, we lugged plastic shovels, colorful buckets, and rakes to the local park's sand box. She dug with the gusto of an archaeologist discovering an ancient fossil. With glee, she proudly raised her pudgy hand to show me her latest treasure. "Look, Mommy, I found a toy car." Sand flew into the air and covered her back, a miniature Indiana Jones.

On the other side of the sand box perched a young, hip mom wearing strappy Coach sandals. Her tyke sported the latest Gymboree gear. She snatched her daughter out of the spray zone and glared my way. "Control your child," she said with an angry scowl.

"She's making a big mess."

Isn't that why we bring them to the park?

"Um…sure," I said to Ms. Vogue. To Ashley, toes buried deep in the pit, "Try to keep the sand in the box, OK?"

"Sure, Mommy," she said, a smile on her face.

Even a trip to McDonald's prompted a fastidious mother to heap on her two cents. Ashley entered the Golden Arches with a glint in her eye and headed straight toward the ball pit. Like an Olympic athlete, she took a nosedive and tossed the balls with abandon.

"Whoopee!" she said with a wide grin as a rainbow of colors bounced around the enclosure.

I ordered two Happy Meals and waited at the front counter. Another mom sidled up to me, pointing at the ball pit.

"Is that your daughter in the purple shirt?" she said with a frown.

"Yep," I said, avoiding eye contact.

"She's throwing balls out of the pit," she said, rolling her eyes. "She's going to hurt someone."

Plastic balls woman!

By the time the subdivision pool opened for summer, my parenting confidence was shot. All the other moms seemed to have kids that played in a careful, controlled manner.

Maybe I didn't know what I was doing? Was something wrong with me? Or worse yet, my kid?

Playgroup met each Monday at 11:00 AM at the neighborhood pool, early enough to make it back home for an afternoon nap. Lathered in SPF-50 and sporting flip flops, I wheeled a cart filled with our gear: pool toys, foam swim noodles, goggles, sunscreen, and a Coleman cooler stocked with drinks and snacks to share with the neighborhood kids.

Beach towels draped over my shoulder, I plopped down in the first lounge chair and looked around for our group. I flagged over the moms and we staked out our territory for the next few hours.

I dragged the lounge chair to the edge of the pool, occasionally glancing at the latest *People* magazine in my lap.

In an hour, hundreds of moms flooded the area, dragging kids in babyseats, strollers, and setting up playpens with umbrellas.

Then the moms arrived with older kids. You know the type. Not bothering to look up and check on their preteens, they spent hours chatting with their fashionable friends. Summertime was their opportunity to work on a Coppertone tan. Decked out in metallic swimsuits, bedazzled sandals, and jeweled necklaces, these ladies sat, dipping their professionally manicured toes in the pool, and scooping out water with fake fingernails to sprinkle on their over-processed bodies. *Yeesch!*

One such mother was Miranda, Queen of the Tanners.

"Hey, Mommy, hold this beach ball for me," said Ashley, tossing a neon yellow ball in the air. I snatched it with one hand.

My daughter dog-paddled in the pool toward her best friend. "Lindsey," she shouted, splashing water. "Try to catch me." Ashley scissor-kicked in a different direction, frantic to put some distance between her and her friend. A mini-tsunami ensued.

"Excuse me," Miranda said, looking up from her throne. "Can you ask your daughter to stop splashing?"

And then the mother of all meltdowns brewed from the pit of my stomach and rumbled up my throat searching for a release.

"In case you forgot, this is a POOL," I spewed, hand on hip. "If you sit near the water, you're going to get wet." I stared her down good. "IF YOU DON'T WANT TO GET WET, THEN GET OUT OF THE DANG POOL!"

Frightened eyes stared back. She pushed herself up from the side of the pool with her arm and seized her gaudy sandals. She mumbled something unintelligible that sounded like, "jerk."

Just like that, the beach ball "slipped" out of my grasp and landed with a resounding plop in the pool at her feet. Water splattered her face, smeared her makeup, and droplets dangled from her designer sunglasses.

"Oops," I said, shrugging my shoulders.

Queen Miranda stormed off, spilling her frozen drink down her leg.

That's right. Just keep moving.

At that moment, I felt like Supermom. I stood up, tossed my head in the air, and smiled. Sand boxes, ball pits, and pools are for kids, not fussy, bored moms. I'd earned this chance to play with my daughter. So what if Ashley's a little more energetic, or excitable. If you can't stand the heat, get out of the pool!

GETTING TO KNOW MY SON ONE TOE AT A TIME

Like an experienced potter sculpting clay, I massaged and kneaded the bottoms of my son's feet. Brock melted like a snowman in August and shared his day with me. He recounted tales of his eighth-grade friends, humorous and witty, with amazing detail and enthusiasm. His funny teacher stories cracked me up until my sides hurt.

"Mom, Rod laughed so hard today that chocolate milk sprayed out of his mouth and hit some dude's lunch," he said.

"Gross," I said with a gasp.

"Did I tell you that my teacher touched the shock pen I had on my desk and sent it flying across the room?"

"Oh my God!" I said, eyes wide. "Why did you bring that to class?"

As our conversation progressed, I stared down at his jagged toenails and calloused feet across my lap and tried to remember how I ended up in this position.

As a young child, my son was talkative, and it was easy to communicate with him. In elementary school, he would run to me the minute he heard a new joke.

We held our bellies and rolled on the ground each time he retold it. When he wanted to test out a new magic trick or practice pulling a prank, he would come to me. Even last year, he was not afraid to share his feelings.

Then at age thirteen, puberty snuck up, stole my son, and replaced him with a moody teenager. I longed to find a way to get him to open up again. I remembered a trick my mother used when I was a teen and asked my son to join me in the living room.

"Come sit down for a sec. Check out this new episode of *Pit Boss*," I said and patted a spot for him on the sofa. "Put your feet up, take a load off."

As my son approached the couch, I noted all his physical changes. Acne sprinkled his nose. His voice had deepened and soft, light-colored hairs appeared on his cheeks and upper lip. His shoulders had broadened and the muscles on his arms were more pronounced.

We stood almost eye-to-eye. He paid better attention to his clothes and dressed in the latest fashion—baggy, faded jeans and tees with trendy logos. Fumes from hair gels and cologne lingered in his bathroom after a shower. Overnight, my soft, round, young boy had changed into an angular, lanky teen, with hormones and attitude to boot.

Like a masseuse, I poured moisturizing lotion onto my warm hands as he relaxed and leaned back against a sofa pillow. I applied pressure to the sides of his feet. He exhaled and let out a sigh. This was my chance to encourage a conversation.

He unveiled things about himself that I had forgotten due to his sullen attitude and need for privacy. He told funny, rich stories filled with description and insight. And I learned something about the imaginative mind of a teenage boy.

"Did you know that kids from school were caught counterfeiting?" he said, eyes focused on the TV.

"Are you kidding?" I said as I rubbed his soles.

"Nope. A kid copied money and spent it at school to buy some candy that another kid was selling."

"Oh my gosh."

"The other kid used the money to buy groceries and got caught."

"Wow, that's incredible. What happened next?"

"How should I know?"

Next evening, he complained about sore, achy feet. He carried over a huge tub of cocoa butter hand cream, plopped onto the sofa and threw his hairy legs onto my lap. Smiling, he held up the lotion and asked, "Will you rub my feet?"

Each night, I rotated and pulled his toes upward, and his day unraveled with the precision of a seasoned storyteller. It worked like a charm, just like with my mom and me.

"Did you know I got a girlfriend?" he said.

"No, you never mentioned it. What's her name?"

"Megan, but don't get all weird and ask a bunch of questions. That's all I'm saying."

"And Mom, I hate pot roast. Meat cooked in a pot is gross. Please don't make me eat that for dinner anymore."

By the weekend, his feet were as soft as velour, and I was thrilled with the peeks into my son's mind. I used my fist to knead back and forth along his soles and asked, "Why did you put your old, red basketball shoes next to your gym bag?"

"I'm bringing them to practice for Kevin, one of my

teammates. He showed up at tryouts with regular shoes and it seemed like he couldn't afford another pair. I'm gonna give him mine."

I choked up as I watched him pull on a thick, clean pair of socks and walk out of the room. I had forgotten how caring and sympathetic he could be to others.

Through massaging my son's feet, I discovered he had a terrific sense of humor, compassion, and a strong desire to be understood. All I needed was patience and strong hands to unmask his true feelings.

ONE-UPPED BY EXPERTS

Like Mufasa and Scar in *The Lion King*, my kids' fights were legendary. Despite a three-year age gap, they argued about everything. Feuds like "It's my turn to sit next to Dad," "Stop breathing on me," and "I'm the fastest runner" echoed through our home on a regular basis. No matter what the issue, if they could fight about it, they would.

"Hey, Ashley," said my five-year-old son, Brock, bouncing from foot to foot. "I found a brand-new pencil in the drawer." He gripped it in his tiny fist and strutted closer to wave it in her face.

"Big deal," said Ashley picking off her nail polish. "I can still hold my breath longer. Watch." She puffed up her cheeks and leaned her head back on a bolster. After a minute, she said, "See. Told ya." She smiled and changed the channel to *Lizzie McGuire*, peeking out the corner of her eye to make sure we all were watching.

"Can you do this?" Brock blasted out the longest and the stinkiest fart. She covered her nose with a sofa pillow and fled the room. Brock grabbed the remote and shimmied into the sofa for a marathon session of *Rugrats*.

Seriously, his farting was legendary.

My husband and I attempted to treat our children fairly. We set aside "alone time" with each kid, encouraged them to work out conflicts and focused on their differences, but it was never enough. They wouldn't stop one-upping each other.

When my oldest child, Ashley, turned eight, we realized she needed glasses.

"Honey," I said letting out a loud breath, "Please take your feet off the television screen."

She dropped her legs down but the next time I walked into the room, it was more of the same.

"How many fingers do I have up?" I said from across the room, waving three digits.

"I don't know. One?" she said with a furrowed brow.

Houston, we have a problem. How come I didn't notice this before?

At *Eye Glasses or More*, Dr. Cyclops broke the bad news. "Your daughter needs glasses," he said looking down his nose. "Surprised you didn't notice sooner."

Just come out and say it, Doc. I'm a terrible mom.

A week later, on the drive back home after getting new specks, the teasing started.

"I'm so lucky I get to wear glasses," she said from the backseat with a smirk, cocking her head in her brother's direction to wait for a reaction.

"I want glasses!" he said, whining and kicking the back of the seat.

"Settle down. Don't let her get your goat. Your eyes are fine," I said with a smile, trying to defuse the situation.

Score One: Ashley

Like most kids in the '90s, mine were cuckoo for Cocoa Puffs and needed their fix of General Mills cereal with Sonny the Cuckoo Bird laughing from the front of the box. Parents at the time had no problem calming their kids down with sugary cereal.

After grocery shopping, they laid in wait for me to unload the groceries and snagged a bowl with milk and devoured the chocolaty goodness.

"I love this cereal," my son said, crunching and munching as fast as possible, milk and chocolate bits scattering on the glass tabletop.

"Hey, save some for me," my daughter said, skipping to the table. She snatched the box and poured it straight into her mouth.

At daybreak, my son stomped into the kitchen, hauled down the popcorn bowl, and reached for the Cocoa Puffs.

What's this? Empty box? Inconceivable.

The racket started as a whine and accelerated to a full-fledged shriek.

"Mom! Where's the Cocoa Puffs?" he said, face sweaty and contorted. "She ate the whole box."

He proceeded to push aside every cardboard box in the pantry in search of the crunchy treat.

After the search and rescue mission, he detected an empty box with the remnants of a Cuckoo bird peeking out from the trash can.

Outwitted again.

Score Two: Ashley

~~~~~

Holidays encourage outrageous one-upping among

adults and kids alike. Ours were no exception. Code black behavior ruled, especially during the most over-rated holiday of them all, Mother's Day.

In those days, my husband shopped at the mall with the kids and together they presented me with one gift, usually something to wear or read.

"Thank you both for the lovely perfume," or "Perfect. I always need another pair of slippers."

But lately, they have chosen to give separate gifts.

"Hey guys," my husband yelled. "It's time for mom to open her gifts."

They flooded into the living room bearing extravagantly wrapped packages. I oohed and aahed over each.

"Oh, these coasters are lovely," I said as I smiled lovingly and touched its surface. "Thanks, Ashley."

My son handed me a wildly wrapped box, festooned with yards of ribbon. I ripped open the wrappings and said, "This bracelet is beautiful. I can't wait to wear it."

"Oops, I'll be right back," he announced and returned in a flash, beaming ear to ear, holding a second package.

What's this? Another gift?

My daughter melted as she watched the proceedings.

"Hey," she said pursing her lips. "I thought we had an agreement. What's this?"

My son hugged me and left the room.

Score Three: Brock

~~~~~~

This year, gift-giving aside, their one-upping extended to their card as well. Together, they handed me one card. On the right-side, in bold cursive, I read aloud, "Happy Mother's Day. You're the greatest. Love, Ashley."

"Thanks, Ashley," I said as I leaned over to hug her.

Then I read the other side of the card. "You are the quintessential mother. You instilled in me a passion that burns like a fire to go forth and accomplish great things." On and on and on it gushed. Then, "Love, Brock."

I asked my daughter, "Who signed this first?"

"Isn't obvious?" she said clenching her jaw. "I did!" She marched out of the room, throwing Brock a side-eye.

Like a kid reaching for the last slice of pie, my son's smile radiated across the room.

Score Four: Brock

GROWING UP IN THE LAUNDRY ROOM

"Who wears all these clothes?" I shouted. Tripping and falling face first onto a smelly load of dirty laundry wasn't an ideal way to start the morning. As I hoisted myself up by leaning on my elbow, soiled underpants stuck on my pinky. I yanked off the briefs and scanned the room in wonder. Mountains of laundry obscured the floor.

Time to recruit a little help with the never-ending mounds of stinky belongings before my temper erupted like an inflamed pimple. I examined my family and wondered who was best suited to sort, fold, and organize piles of mismatched socks, pajama tops with missing bottoms, and men's underwear?

I scrutinized my nine-year-old daughter from head to toe, appraising Ashley like an automobile dealer sizing up a car. Sturdy, high levels of energy, upbeat. She would do nicely, efficient as a compact convertible. Plus, my golden-haired preteen showed signs of wanting more duties around the house.

"Sweetie, are you still interested in earning some

money?" I asked my perky, pony-tailed fifth-grader. She jerked her head in my direction, green eyes ablaze with excitement.

"What do I have to do?"

"I need a hand folding laundry," I said.

We worked out a deal, starting at fifty cents a load, negotiating up to ten dollars per week. Little did she know that we have eighty-nine loads every seven days.

Her desire to make some cash and her interest in new chores made her the only logical choice. With my husband's track record, I didn't even consider him. Just last month, he washed the infamous one load, each item squeezed as tight as pickles in a jar, detergent stuck on everything. Large towels, delicate bras, reds, and bright whites, why bother to separate? I dismissed my six-year-old son. He couldn't be counted on to put his dirty duds in the basket, let alone wash them. Ashley remained my number one choice, beating out the male competition.

For weeks, she proved to be a diligent helper, very enthusiastic, and thorough. I took this opportunity to teach her the value of teamwork. I explained that with her support I could talk on the phone without multitasking and cook dinner without stopping to finish another load. With my extra time, we could play Jenga, talk about boys, and discuss math homework. It seemed to be the solution to my overload. She got paid and received extra attention. Everyone benefited.

Each night, Ashley folded laundry intent on doing her best. At every opportunity, I bragged about her prowess to friends and relatives.

"She's doing terrific. A great help to me," I said on the phone as Ashley smiled in the background. "Folds wash, never complains, so efficient."

She hoarded her change in a small box. One morning she counted and recounted her earnings. "Yep, I earned $10 this week, just folding laundry," she said to a friend on the phone, "Want to go to the mall?"

She learned the value of saving for the things she needed. A note prominently hung on her bedroom door, listed tank tops, capris, bangle bracelets, and more. She even clipped store ads for PacSun and Forever 21. She learned the difference between a want and a need.

"Mom, if I buy these jeans that I need, I have extra left over for the gold charm bracelet."

Monday arrived, with more than six loads of men's undershirts, briefs, and black socks waiting for Ashley's attention. As I dumped out the dry fluffy mass, I felt her melting like a chocolate bar on hot asphalt.

"Mom, I can't do this anymore. It's just too much. I can't go from doing nothing to all this," she said. "Tell the guys to take off their underwear the right way or I'm folding it inside out."

Oh no, mutiny! My plan to teach responsibility and maintain my newfound freedom from folding clothes unraveled. I listened to all of her complaints until she calmed down. I explained it was a high-volume day because Dad just returned from a ten-day trip.

"Can I get a little help here?" she whined, analyzing the big pile at her feet.

To reach a compromise, I suggested that on busy days her brother could fold towels while she supervised. After ten minutes, she was back on track and only mumbled complaints under her breath. I sipped coffee, leaned back and let out a sigh.

Laundry continued to cycle through our household at the hectic pace of doughnuts flying down the chute at

Krispy Kreme. Ashley even took the initiative to put the wet wash in the dryer and asked, "Mom, do you want me to start a load?" As I watched her fold clean clothes without complaint, her level of maturity thrilled me, all as a result of her latest chore.

She took personal satisfaction in completing a full basket. If someone offered to assist, she declared, "This belongs to me. I'm trying to earn some extra money here. Go do something else."

I peeked into her bedroom as she folded wash, stacked dishrags, and rolled socks together, lost in thought.

"Mom, how did you have time to do all this laundry?" she laughed. "You should have asked me sooner. Need a helping hand with dinner?"

I leaned over with misty eyes, gave her a quick pat on the back, and smiled as I sat down to help her. I realized that she was on track to become an amazing young lady who understands the beauty of cooperation, the importance of keeping Mom happy, and the thrill of earning her own dough.

SMOKIN' HOT SUMMER VACATION

"Walking distance to the ocean" promised *TripAdvisor.com*. With a press of the "request booking" key, I purchased three nights at Cove Condos based on the owner's promise, "spectacular ocean view, comfortable furniture, and smell of ocean breezes from the comfort of your living room. Outdoor patio surrounded by bougainvillea."

San Clemente, here we come!

Up until this point, my search for available rentals during the Labor Day weekend proved fruitless. Hotels in California filled up faster than the San Francisco Giant's stadium during playoffs.

Book it now, my head screamed.

Once we flung open the front door, it was apparent that our townhouse rental was not as described.

"Got to be kidding," I said to my husband, slumping over slightly. "We've been scammed."

I stared in vain at the peeling paint, crumbled walkway, and dismal landscaping. In our hurry, I neglected to check Yelp. Too late, I scrolled through mostly one-star reviews like "Smells like wet dog. Disappointed," and "This place is a pit. Our room was filthy, old food left on dresser. Stay away."

God help us.

Due to our late arrival, the owner hid the keys for us in the front door mailbox, rusty and clinging for life by one measly screw.

"This place is so dated and small," Mike said. "Nothing else available for miles, right?"

We hauled our bags inside and picked out a spot to plop. One king-sized bed filled the living room edge to edge. The space from the front door to the mattress was about three feet, enough to make a temporary bed out of extra blankets for the kiddos.

"Guys, it's going to be cozy tonight," said Mike, scanning the room. "Kids, grab a few blankets and make a bed between the door and the mattress."

"Burrrr, I'm freezing," said Ashley, my pony-tailed ten-year-old, hugging her jacket around her body. "Can we turn on the heat?"

We'd been warned that the temperature took a huge dip in the evenings in California and we came prepared with hoodies and sweatshirts.

I located the thermostat on the wall nearest the bathroom. A hastily scrawled Post-It note stated, "To operate the heat, turn the right knob to the desired temperature and press the 'Go' button."

I adjusted it to seventy-two degrees and waited. A hiss and a kabang rattled across the room.

After ten minutes my daughter complained, "Mom, it's still freezing."

"Give it ten more minutes," I said, fingers crossed. "Needs some time to warm up."

We cranked on the television for the late news and snuggled deep into the covers together.

"It's so cold in here," I said to Mike, poking him in the ribs. "Go see if you can figure out the thermostat."

My husband turned the knob to seventy-five degrees and pressed the button again. Nothing. No subtle click, not even a loud bang this time.

My son turned down the television when we heard three knocks on the door.

"Who the heck's that?" said Mike, cutting his eyes toward the door. He pulled open the door one inch at a time.

"Hey, my family is staying in the condo next door," said a short, tubby man wearing nothing but nylon running shorts, his chest hair glistening with sweat. "Do you have any idea how to turn down the heat?"

Is that steam coming off his body?

"We're having problems, too, except our place is freezing."

"Well, it's so hot I'm sleeping on the porch. My family's inside with the front door opened to get a little air. Sorry to bother you."

"No problem. I called the landlord," Mike said, propping the door with his foot. "Hopefully, he'll repair it in the morning."

He shut the door and said, "Sorry guys, we're going to have to make do. Sleep in your sweatshirt and grab another blanket."

The next morning as we prepared to leave for the beach, someone knocked on the door again.

"I'm the landlord, Debbie," she said in a loud voice. "Did you call?"

"Glad you're here. We were freezing all night. How

do we work the furnace?"

Debbie marched over to the wall, sighed and spun the dial.

"Did you touch this?" she said, clenching her jaw. Her eyes circled the room daring someone to admit to this violation.

"Yep, we were freezing," Mike said matter-of-factly, hands on hips.

"You were controlling the neighbor's heat. Didn't you see the note?"

In a flash, she ripped off the Post-It note to expose another note underneath, "For Condo Unit #2."

"Are you kidding? How were we supposed to figure that out?"

"Pretty simple," she said, pointing across the room. "Your thermostat is the one on the other wall."

Conveniently situated in the closet near the floor. How could we miss it?!

We learned one thing from our experience; plan early, check Yelp, and read Post-It notes carefully. You never know if your neighbor is the Wolfman.

MAMA'S HUNGRY

I'm not sure when I started hiding thin mint Girl Scout cookies in tampon boxes. It was somewhere between the time my daughter took her first steps and my husband's renewed interest in dieting. It was like candy contraband.

Stop judging me.

Like most problems, it started out slowly like an unripened avocado. For days, it's ready to chip your teeth and then you blink, it's brown and ready for the trash.

Let me get this out here first.

Did you know that two-thirds of moms have a secret stash of goodies kept hidden from the family?

Think about that.

It makes sense. Moms are destined to get the last bite of cake, the last sip of diet Coke, the last cookie crumble.

Mama's hungry!

I perfected my sneaky habit when my first child transitioned from baby food in jars to solids on plates. When she turned two years old, I realized I had to fend for myself if I wanted a fair share of junk food.

When she was just a tot, I squirreled away the candy and pastries on a shelf higher than her chubby arms could reach, about three feet.

Once our little girl distinguished the difference between broccoli and cupcakes, I had to refine my strategy.

As the years passed, I moved my sugary inventory higher and further to the back of the shelf.

"Mommy, look what I found," my four-year-old daughter said with a huge grin on her face. "Chocolate-chip cookies. Stuck in the way back."

Drats!

Twelve years later and my two teenagers surpassed me in weight and stature.

"Hey guys, it's time to measure you," I said with a pencil as I prepared to mark their height on the door frame.

Five-foot-ten? For the love of Pete.

I fell even lower on the food chain and it was three against one, including my husband. If I didn't set a bit aside to eat after I set the table, dispersed the condiments, poured drinks, and delivered seconds, I would starve.

"We have any sweets?" my hubby asked after dinner. "I could go for Pepperidge Farm Milan cookies. Even Nilla Wafers would do."

"Nope," I said, trying not to look him in the eye. "We eat too much junk food."

What happened to the diet?

As for non-chocolaty treats, my gang gobbled down Twizzlers red licorice the moment the bag smacked the counter.

Whap.

I retaliated and developed a taste for black licorice. This I could leave sprawled on the kitchen table, untouched.

"Gross. Why'd you buy the yucky licorice?" my son said, eyes all scrunched up. "We hate it."

"Seriously?" I said slapping my hands to my cheeks. "Thought it was your favorite."

My plan was progressing nicely.

Soon I grew to "love" Bryer's coconut ice cream, Vienna fingers, brown sugar oatmeal, hummus, green peppers, and pomegranates too.

Like a special ops military maneuver, I camouflaged the sweet stuff, like Oreos and M&Ms, deep into decoy cereal boxes of Grape Nuts. No one opened that crap.

As far as drinks go, don't judge me because I love soda. In the vegetable bins beneath lettuce and a bundle of carrots, I stashed cans of the cola.

Who eats vegetables?

Then one evening, as the kids zoned out over *Drake & Josh*, I spilled my little dirty secret with my husband.

"Shhhh," I whispered as I motioned with my finger for him to follow me. "Don't say a word. I hid brownies under the dresser in our bedroom. Want some?"

"You really have to ask?" he said sniffing the air.

The anticipation of gooey, rich, chocolaty brownies cast him under a spell. He tiptoed behind me and up the steps.

Are we still talking about the same thing?

In unison, my kids' heads snapped in our direction. "Gross," they said and turned back to the television.

"Hurry up," I said to Mike. "Shut the door."

I jumped on the bed and threw him a fork.

"Do you feel guilty not sharing with the kids?" I said as I attempted to wolf down a pan of iced brownies.

"What kids?" he said and laughed like a hyena.

HELICOPTER MOM

It was simply too tempting. My son's sophomore English essay lay plopped on the floor outside his bedroom door. What would it hurt to take a little peek?

Back when Brock was in elementary school, parents probably considered me a helicopter mom. You know that overinvolved mother…err…smotherer who paid entirely too much attention to her kids' homework, sports activities, and friendships. Like a helicopter, she constantly circled overhead.

That was me.

My "problem" started in full force around the time my son was in first grade. I really messed things up.

Mental math reigned supreme that year. In its simplest form, it's a tactic used by teachers to help students to learn how to mentally add numbers together without the use of paper, pencil, and calculator. Strategies like rounding up numbers five or over and rounding down numbers under five are utilized. For instance, when adding twelve plus nineteen you mentally hear in your head ten plus twenty. The answer's thirty.

Boring.

My son's math skills excelled other first graders.

Mental math? Phish, posh. That was for the ordinary kids.

After school, he spread out his homework on the kitchen table. I prepared dinner as he munched on string cheese and pretzel sticks. I glanced at his current homework, appalled by the assignment.

"Wow," I said, rolling my eyes and staring at the "dumb" homework. "Can you add fifty-two plus eleven?" I asked him.

"Yep, that's easy, Mom," he said leaning back in his chair with a playful grin. "It's sixty-three."

"Do you need to use mental math?"

"Mrs. Strickman said we have to use it for this assignment."

"But you can do all this in your head, right?" I said, eyeballing his anxious face.

"No problem," he said. A smile curled his lips.

"Then do the homework the way you know how to do it," I said with a satisfied grin. "Pencil in the real answers."

Mental math? Come on!

But my plan backfired. After school, as I waited in the carpool lane, my son stormed toward my car, marching with the determination of the Virginia Corps of Cadets.

Left. Left. Left, right, left.

"Look what you did," he said, throwing his homework assignment on my lap as he buckled into the backseat. "It's all your fault. I got an F!" he sniffled, holding back tears.

"I'm so sorry. But I knew you could add without mental math. I thought the assignment was stupid. Pinky swear, I won't interfere again," I said, dangling

my pinky over the back of the headrest. But I couldn't stop myself.
Mom knows best. Right!?
I interceded in ways too numerous to count. If the teacher accepted messy illegible homework, I ripped it to shreds and insisted he start over. When students were asked to volunteer five hours, he signed up for six. *See what I mean? I'm overinvolved.*

By the time he entered high school, I curbed my helicopter mom ways. I had read enough books and online websites to understand the dangers of overinvolved parenting. After all, I didn't want him to end up like one of those weird homeschooled kids.

Hey, I reassured myself, he can't take you to college. It was time for him to be accountable for his own failure or success, and he didn't need my constant input.

Yet, that day I spied a pile of typewritten papers neatly stacked outside my son's bedroom door, the temptation was too much. It begged to be picked up. Alas, I longed to see what my kid had been doing at school.

For four years I avoided getting involved with his homework. He seemed to be doing an admirable job. Our policy, as long as the report card grades were up to snuff, Dad and I wouldn't interfere, especially me.

I rushed to my computer then glanced at the clock on the screen. The digital clock shined midnight.

I smiled as I read his history paper. Great beginning. *He must get the funny opening from his mom.* Paragraphs adequately formulated. Spelling clear. No glaring grammar issues.

Wait a minute! Since when is Michelangelo spelled with an "a" at the end? That's not right.

I thumbed through his papers at breakneck speed. Oh god. Oh god. He misspelled Michelangelo a total of twenty-seven times. This is bad. Real bad.

There is no way he can turn this in with twenty-seven mistakes.

So, I edited and corrected all the Michelangelo misspellings.

To ensure that I caught every single one, I started back at the first paragraph. Then I found other errors. *You cannot use a semi-colon that way. Dear Lord, a period always goes inside a quotation mark. A bibliography needs to be alphabetized.*

I couldn't stop.

A sentence should never end with a preposition.

Is it too late to rewrite the whole paper?

After an hour or eighty-nine corrections later, his paper was perfect.

I reprinted, restapled, and set it outside his bedroom door then shredded the original essay.

He'll never know the difference.

In the morning, I tapped on his bedroom door. "Hey, would you like pancakes and bacon for breakfast?"

"Um, sure. I'm so tired. I worked on that stupid paper all night. I hope Mr. Grimm appreciates my hard work," said Brock.

"I'm sure it's great," I said, nodding my head.

"I was lucky to get it in on time. I had to run plagtracker.com before midnight for full credit."

"Come again?"

"A plagiarism checker for the teacher. You know, in case someone cheats. Then it's time-stamped."

"That's a good idea. I heard high school kids are doing a lot of cheating these days."

"Yep. If you make any changes after midnight, you get an automatic zero. She's going to compare the website with the actual print-outs we turn in today."

"Have a great day," I said, wiping the sweat from my brow. "See you after school."

How the hell does the teacher have time to do that? What about the budget cuts they keep carping about?

As he drove off, I called my husband at work.

"Holy shit," I said, sweat dripping down my cleavage. "I changed Brock's English essay. HE'S GOING TO GET IN BIG TROUBLE."

"Slow down. What did you do?"

My homework meddling story rolled out one awful detail at a time.

"Let's ride it out," he said. "No way that young teacher has time to check thirty-five kid's reports. Wait for the grades to be posted online. If he gets an F, then go in and explain."

Weeks passed. Then two months. By that time, we received the semester report cards. With trembling hands, I ripped open the envelope.

Running my finger down the row, I spotted English. *I earned an A.*

TO CATCH A THIEF

Sleep, punctuated by a "kapow" and "yelp," caused my husband and me to leap out of bed, Ninja style. Without hesitation, I nabbed the clock radio to use as a weapon and my husband grabbed his glasses. We stood in ready position, left foot forward, and right leg prepared to swing up and out to smack an assailant.

Cowabunga dude.

I tilted my head toward thundering footsteps charging up the staircase. Thump, bump, "help." Our bedroom door flew open with a whoop. In flowery pajama bottoms stood our teenage daughter with mascara-lined eyes and disheveled hair.

"Two guys are outside my window with a ladder trying to break in," she cried, hobbling into our bedroom on one leg, eyes crazy. "I tripped up the steps trying to get to you," she said, holding her ankle with the opposite hand.

"Be quiet," I said, yanking her down to the floor. I pulled up the shades an inch and cracked the window open. "Let's try to catch them."

Floodlights surrounded our property and enabled me to take a quick peek around the front yard from the second-floor window. I scanned right and left. Not a soul in sight. *What had she seen?*

"Let's watch for awhile before we call the police," I said, pushing my shoulders back. "Mike, go out the back door, creep around to the front, and grab 'em."

"Come again?" he said, frowning. "You want me to go outside?"

"Hurry. Maybe we can startle them. I'll watch and wait from the window." I turned to my daughter and added, "Go with Dad."

With my loved-ones off to catch a burglar, I mulled over the chain of events. Hmmm, a ladder? Two guys? Something didn't make sense. I'm a pretty light sleeper and hadn't heard a thing.

I unlocked the front door and my husband hustled inside. "Nothing," he said, trying to catch his breath. "I searched the front and back. Zip." He glared at Ashley, "Are you positive you saw something?"

"Yep. Two guys with a ladder were definitely breaking into my room."

"Let's check her room," I said. Ashley's legs quaked as we entered her bedroom on the first floor.

"Turn the lights off," I told my husband. "Let's look at it from her perspective."

Yowza!

When closed, the sheer fabric shades in my daughter's room provided the necessary privacy. However, on the night of the "attempted break-in," they had not been properly closed and light from the street lamp entered through the layers of fabric, creating a pattern of shadowy stripes on the walls. Also, the wind bent the trees and created creepy shadows that danced around the walls like a scene in a horror movie.

She must be nuts to sleep in here!
"Tell me again about this ladder," I asked.
As she wove her tale, it all came together. Two men. One stands up. A ladder.
"I got it! You probably saw a deer with antlers. You startled a buck nibbling on grass outside your windows and he reared his antlers up, hence the ladder effect."
"No way. I didn't have my glasses on but I saw two guys trying to break in with a ladder." Her gaze bounced between her father and me. "When I shined my iPhone light at them, they ran off."
An iPhone light as self-defense? Genius!
"Can I sleep with you?" she begged, holding me in her radar lock.
Giving in to her request, I shared a bed with a tooth-grinding, cover-kicking, warm-bodied teen
In the morning, we heard a slight rustling beneath the open bedroom window. I snuck a peek and sure enough, foraging under our daughter's windowsill was a full-grown buck with antlers.
Run, deer, run. Don't look into the light.

I NEED MORE BANDWIDTH

Last week my daughter's return from college should have elicited great fanfare, something akin to trumpets announcing the coming of the Queen. When she was away, I missed her sunny personality and positive attitude. Usually when she hits the door, I wave my hands like a maniac and say, "Hey, how you doing? You hungry? Want to watch a movie? Need any money? So glad you're home!"

But not this time.

When I peeked out the front window, I panicked. She stood on our porch steps, arms akimbo as she juggled college junk and a stack of mobile equipment: laptop computer and iPhone in one arm and an iPad in the other.

What the hell?

I considered blocking her entry. Our household simply couldn't handle any more computer paraphernalia and still maintain adequate bandwidth. My husband informed me that bandwidth controlled the rate of data transfer, measured in bits per second.

Whatever.

"Hi sweetie," I said to Ashley sucking in a deep

breath. "What ya got there?"
This can't be happening.
Let me explain.

Since she's been at college, my hubby, son, and I have battled it out like Hulk Hogan vs. the Undertaker. We each struggled to maintain the upper hand. It was to my advantage to achieve and maintain the strongest computer connection. It was a battle to the blood, and I'd suffered one cross-face cradlepin maneuver too many.

Before her return, computer access was as inadequate as trying to operate the space station from a telephone booth.

We didn't have problems in our previous house, a typical two-story with a living room, kitchen, dining room, and office on the first floor and bedrooms upstairs. However, our current residence featured as many zigzags as the Winchester Mystery House. On the main floor, a central staircase off the foyer shot up to the second floor, pretty basic. But one bedroom, built on an addition, extended into the backyard and the den attached to the side of the house. To get to these rooms from the front foyer, you needed to make two rights and a left. These twists and turns yielded sketchy Internet on a good day.

Upstairs, a wall separated my son's bedroom from my office nook. Most days, I wrote uninterrupted from 8:00 AM until school got out around 3:00 PM. I cringed each afternoon when I heard the garage door creek open. Regularly, my son returned with a handful of testosterone-laden seventeen-year-old boys ready to do combat with the latest Xbox 360 game, like Assassin's Creed IV, Black Flag, or Call of Duty: Advanced Warfare.

Bye, bye Internet, nice knowing you.

"Mom, the guys and I are hanging out in my room for a couple of hours to play Xbox, okay?" my son said.

What I heard sounded like, "My gang of loud friends is going to ruin your Internet power within five minutes, okay?"

Aargguh!

For hours on the other side of the wall, teenagers with husky voices yelled out foul language as they combatted each other in a violent video game. Strange guttural sounds emanated through the plasterboard. *Grunt, burp, capow, ouch, oof.*

On my side of the wall, with shaky hands, I attempted to type a full sentence in email before being dropped from the Comcast server.

Dangnabbit.

With their robust Internet service, I even overheard them use FaceTime from their iPhone to talk to their girlfriends and watch YouTube videos.

Come on!

In frustration, I grabbed *The Tiny Book of Patience: Practical Tips for Becoming a More Patient Parent* and snuggled down in a recliner until dinnertime when the gang left with the promise of a hot meal from their mamas.

To make matters worse, one day a week, Mike worked from home, his office conveniently situated directly below my second floor nook. His computer access, strong as a bull elephant, displayed nary a blip in connection. I heard him humming away as his Internet juice whirled, happily working simultaneously on two computers, an iPhone, and iPad.

He's hogging all my bandwidth!

Working in the loft above him, I covertly wrestled against Mike for the ultimate power. I attempted to sabotage his Internet as I rebooted, restarted, and shut down the computer.

Home network be damned!

After one hour of being dropped and left hanging, I pushed my work-in-progress aside and hung my head over the desk. "Hey," I hollered down the staircase. "Do you have Internet connection?"

"Yep, working fine," he said, tapping on the keyboard. "You?"

"Nothin'. Can you turn off some of your other devices? Maybe pick either the iPad or the computer. You're killing me up here. Keep getting dropped."

Finally, I called it quits. "I give up," I said. My irritation simmered below the surface. "What do you want for dinner?" I stormed down the staircase and grimaced his way. "You win," I said over my shoulder.

So, when my daughter returned home from college, I'd reached the final straw. I would bide my time until she left then call the experts at Comcast, our Internet provider. Enough was enough. Was it too much to hope for Internet connection to last longer than fifteen minutes? Why couldn't I use both the iPhone and email? Was I asking too much?

Comcast dispatched Jose, a techno-angel bearing a massive toolbox and coils of cables.

"What's the problem?" he said as he entered the front door.

"My internet sucks. I'm dropped repeatedly and can't maintain strong bandwidth."

"Let me take a look around at your home network." He paced the house, taking notes, and scrunching his forehead.

"Here's the problem. Your router is located in the den. The wireless cable must pass through the kitchen to get to the upper floor. That's bad."

Whatever you say. You're the expert. Stop talking and get to work.

"Too much metal. Your microwave, refrigerator, and stove prevent a solid connection. For the best service the router needs to be closer to your nook."

Say no more! Hop to it, Computer Man.

He toiled to install the router and necessary gear closer to my computer. After all, I justified, I'm home 24/7. I'm a writer.

"That should do the trick," he said with a flick of his wrist. "Go test it yourself."

I rushed to my desktop computer and experienced the magical moment, lightning-fast Internet.

"You're a genius. I can't repay you enough. Here take this pan of brownies. Want a Coke? How about cash?"

After he left, I zoomed upstairs to my lair. Click, click. Opened email. Click, click. Opened Facebook. With a few more clicks, I opened YouTube and Twitter.

That evening Mike retired into the living room and unloaded a massive briefcase filled with computer equipment. "Hey, what's going on?" he said, pressing keys like mad. "Internet's slow."

About that time, my son and his friend started to holler. "Mom, my friends can't use their phones up here and Xbox isn't working. What's wrong?"

"Well, forgot to tell you the good news. Comcast Guy relocated the router upstairs and it's never been better...for me."

Ha, ha, now I have the power.

YOUNG ENTREPRENEUR

Here's what I know for sure about parenting: there will be chaos, you'll make questionable decisions, and a sense of humor goes a long way.

My husband and I attempted to teach our kids about the value of money. Sayings like, "Money doesn't grow on trees," "A penny saved is a penny earned," and "We're not made of money" were frequently echoed in our home.

We believed that kids get greater satisfaction earning their own money in order to spend it on the things they wanted.

Get a job, kid.

By fifth grade, our son distributed flyers door-to-door to wash cars, mow grass, walk dogs, tutor math, and babysit the brats, anything to make a few bucks. Piles of leaflets cluttered the kitchen counter and were taped haphazardly to the refrigerator door.

One day I found cash in his jeans.

"Where'd you get the five dollars?" I asked Brock.

"I sell kids donuts from the bakery before school."

"Good idea," I said.

A regular Warren Buffett.

Soon he brainstormed for ways to make larger gains.

He designed a marshmallow gun and perfected the prototype for weeks.

From across the living room, he loaded and aimed at his sister.

"Mom, make him stop," Ashley said swatting at the air. "Brock keeps smacking me in the face with marshmallows."

"It's ready," he said giving me the thumbs up sign. He stowed the gun under his armpit and strutted out of the room.

For his latest project, he asked with a worried expression, "Can I borrow some seed money?"

How the heck does he know what that means?

"Sure, but I need to be paid back after your first sale."

"Deal," he said.

After shopping at Home Depot, he dumped bags of supplies onto the garage floor: duct tape, fittings, and PVC pipe in assorted sizes.

"You need to keep track of your expenses," I said, staring at the mess. "Then you'll know much profit you made."

For cheap labor, he rounded up a willing gang of adolescent workers and started an assembly line to build marshmallow guns in our garage.

An at-home sweatshop.

In addition to heaps of plastic pipes, sticky splotches covered our garage floor making parking inside impossible.

To encourage him, Dad was his first customer, buying ten guns to give to his employees as stress relievers.

Later Brock used the cash from sales to start his next endeavor, selling cheap, colorful plastic watches popular with the middle school girls. Loot arrived monthly from China and India in beat-up packages.

I pictured my son wearing a hundred wristwatches on his arm like a New York street corner hawker.

By age sixteen, he opted to spend his cash on looking cool instead of electronic gadgets.

"Can I get Jordans?" he asked.

"That's out of our price range," I said. "If you want them bad enough, you'll have to buy them yourself."

He secured a job in the cafeteria before school making the burritos and other breakfast goods. Plus, on weekends he refereed basketball.

In no time, his hard work paid off. He had enough money to buy the precious sneakers he desired, and overnight he became a Sneakerhead, one of those guys who collected limited or rare sneakers. His room overflowed with boxes stacked past the windowsill.

During basketball season, our young entrepreneur sold knock-off NBA Jerseys. If the Warriors were your favorite team, what size did you need?

"Hey Mom, can you bring a bunch of the jerseys to school today?"

"Sure, I'll swing by on my way to the grocery store."

The next thing I know, I'm in the school parking lot surrounded by twenty-five teenage boys with the trunk up.

This is a bad idea.

In an instant, I'd gone from quiet suburban mom to that guy who sells bootleg shirts outside the Coliseum before the football game.

The things we do for our kids.

Despite tripping over boxes, stepping on marshmallows, and rendering our garage useless, we're proud of our son's accomplishments and entrepreneurial spirit. He understood that it takes hard work and ingenuity to earn money, and sneakers don't fall from trees.

YOU ARE MY FAVORITE

Go ahead and say it. Deep down you have a favorite child. One kid is easier to be around, never whiny or cranky. This child is happy, obedient, and listens better. For me that child was the oldest, my daughter. The favorite.

As an infant, she was beautiful, cheerful, and a great sleeper to boot. When people would visit, they'd rush to her side.

"Can I hold her?" they begged, reaching down into her crib with greedy hands, ready to plant a smooch on her face or squeeze her plump cheeks.

I'd place her in their arms and she would "coo" and "ahh," happy to be held. She was our perfect angel.

From toddlerhood through high school, our smiley, pony-tailed daughter got along with all her friends, and teachers would send positive reports like, "Her attitude is superb" and "She's an asset in our class."

Once she started college, we became best friends. She knew the right thing to say to brighten my day.

"Mom, thanks for always being there," she said touching my arm. "Some of my friend's moms are never home. You're the greatest."

She guided the rest of the family in fun activities, a party planner in the making.

"We should go bowling tonight," she said, bouncing on her toes.

"Want to go to the beach?"

"Doesn't it sound like fun to go to Disneyland in June?"

She never ran out of ideas for family time.

All was at peace in our home until she didn't get her way.

"Let's go to the Cheesecake Factory for lunch," said The Favorite, reaching down to scratch our dog, Stanley. He rewarded her with a lick on the wrist.

"Nah," said the rest of us in unison. "We ate there last weekend. Let's go someplace else."

With a switch of her blond mane, she turned her back on us and stormed away. "God!" she mumbled from the other room.

"Gosh, what does it matter?" said my sixteen-year-old son, rolling his eyes. "I only want to spend time together. And it's not fair that she always gets to pick."

And just like that, my athletic, green-eyed son was my new favorite, the second child. Like a typical second child, he was a flexible people-pleaser. He learned early on that life doesn't always go his way. His sense of humor connected our family. He had a way with a silly joke or a funny rap song to lighten the mood.

"What do you call a boy who finally stood up to the bullies?" he said. "An ambulance."

I held my belly as tears leaked out of my eyes.

When he walked into the kitchen before mealtime, I could count on him to know just the right thing to say.

"Mom, need any help?"

"Thanks," I said with a heavy sigh. "After dinner, can you do clean up? I have a PTA meeting to get to and don't want to come back to this big mess."

"No problem," he said squeezing my hand. "Count on me."

But his cell phone buzzed between pasta primavera and strawberry cheesecake. He pushed away from the table and charged the back door, tipping a chair over in his excitement to get out.

"Got to go. My friends are waiting outside. Later."

In a flash, he zipped away, leaving a broken promise and stacks of dirty dishes in his wake.

I looked down at Stanley, our three-year-old fluffy white cock-a-chon. He nudged my leg and cocked his head as if to say, "I'm here for you. Let me help."

He's my new favorite.

HUSBANDS

"I'm really here to get away from my husband. He blew out his Achilles tendon playing beer die at my son's fraternity party. In the beginning, I was sympathetic but then I got irritated with the non-stop calls for, "Where's my glasses?," "Water," or "I need meds." Finally, I just stuck it all in a backpack and made him wear it around the house."

—Stacey Gustafson, *Get Your Funny On*, Tommy T's Comedy Club, Pleasanton, California

I NETFLIX CHEATED ON MY HUSBAND

I tried ways to end my deception, but nothing worked. To protect my indiscretion, I routinely deleted my Internet browser history, shredded phone bills, and swore my friends to secrecy. I Netflix cheated on my husband.

How did this begin you ask? I blame it on the old-fashioned dinner-and-a-movie routine. Our choices had boiled down to *The Lego Batman Movie* and *Fifty Shades Darker*. Why were we wasting our money on this crap? So, we traded a night out for a night in.

It all started so innocently.

Cable television options are limitless. Netflix, Amazon Prime, Hulu, HBO Now, the list goes on. No need to go to the theater when you can indulge in more than fifty hours, or five seasons of thirteen episodes. Intriguing shows like *Shooter, Stranger Things, Dexter, It's Always Sunny in Philadelphia,* and *House of Cards* sucked us in faster than a fur ball to a Dust Buster.

Netflix, where've you been my whole life?

We clicked through cable channels and realized we'd only scraped the surface of the Netflix barrel.

On Saturday night, we trolled the channels and found *The Killing*, a crime drama based in Seattle, featuring homicide detective Sarah Linden and her sidekick, Holder. It had more red herrings than a fish farm, and we were addicted by the first hour.

"Man, this is good," I said, after three episodes. "One more."

"No can do," said my husband, shaking his head. "Got to get up early."

"Come on," I said, batting my eyelashes. "Please."

"Fine, one more. But that's it."

Season One, Episode Four, here we come.

By Sunday evening, we squeezed in Episodes Five and Six.

"Got to call it quits now," he said, rubbing his eyes and giving me a glassy stare. "Up for work by six."

"Okay," I said, fidgeting on the sofa. "I'm going stay up a little and read. Night."

"No cheating. We agreed to watch this together."

Think again, sucker.

The glow of the television beckoned. What would it hurt? I slammed shut *The Girl on the Train* and clicked on Episode Seven. I snuggled into my soft throw blanket, popped a can of Coke and let the drama begin. Heck, I'd rewatch it the next time we were together. He'd never know. But I knew I'd crossed the line.

I had become a Netflix cheater.

After he left for work the next day, I thought, "What would it hurt to take a little peek?"

Bam, hooked again, and I binged-watched five more episodes.

Around 6:00 PM, I texted him, "What time you coming home for dinner?"

"Thirty minutes."
Oh crap, he'll be here soon.
"Can you pick up some milk and...umm...pimentos?"
He'll be searching for hours.

I needed to buy some time to finish Season One. I couldn't stand not knowing what was happening. Would they catch the real killer? What's that new evidence they keep talking about?

Suddenly, I detected the slow hum of the garage door. *How the hell did he find the damn pimentos that fast?* With a loud bang, the door clanged shut on the concrete floor. I hit "off" on the remote.

He strolled into the room, and his green eyes scrutinized the screen.

"Were you watching *The Killing*?"

"No way. We promised to watch together."

"Where did we leave off anyway?" he said, trying to trip me up with probing questions. He clicked on the three-way light on the end table next to me.

"Hey, turn that off," I said, holding a hand to cover my eyes. "So bright."

What is this Guantanamo?

"Well?" he asked again.

"I think it's the one where they discover that kid in the teacher's apartment," I said, wiping my sweaty hands on my pants.

"Wrong."

"Um, I'm not sure," I said, as I leaned in and heard the distinct drip of the kitchen faucet. My armpits sweated more than a hot flash.

"Did you watch more episodes?" he said, eyebrows pinched together, as he squeezed in between the arm of the sofa and my body until our thighs touched. "You can trust me. I won't get mad."

"Fine," I blurted out. "I couldn't help it. I Netflix cheated."

Seriously, dude, you've been out of town so much I had to get my fix.

"Why?"

"I'm sorry," I said, staring down at my feet. "It's just so good. Never planned it to go this far."

"Promise not to watch anymore?" he said, cocking his head to one side.

I vowed to keep my promise, turned on the television and started scrolling for something else to watch. We'd considered binging on *Shooter* after watching the previews on Netflix, a drama series based on a former military sniper called back into action to prevent a plot to kill the President.

But when I clicked on it, I noticed that the red bar underneath, the one that indicated if it had been recently viewed, had disappeared.

What?! Holy cow, he's Netflix cheated on me!

I lost all sense of remorse and settled in for hours of binging on *Shooter*. Two can play this game.

Redecorating Do Us Part

Back when we were newlyweds, my husband and I daydreamed about buying our first home and ways to decorate. But as we scoured the used furniture stores and discount department stores, I realized our tastes didn't align.

In the '90s, my style gravitated toward flea market chic, like Monica on *Friends*. I envisioned patterned wallpaper in wide stripes and bold primary colors would adorn my walls with accents of frilly floral pillows, comforters, and curtains to complete the coordinated look. Think wicker furniture, pleated lampshades, and rag-rolled walls. No surface would be untouched by my decadent, overdone decorating sense.

In contrast, Mike's design aesthetic leaned toward early college dorm. Think plastic milk crates, posters, and waterbeds.

Low budget décor.

After three years of marriage, we moved to Atlanta. Once we unpacked the moving boxes, I dressed up our bedroom with yellow floral curtains and matching comforter. Rolls of striped coordinating wallpaper stood like sentries at the foot of our bed ready to be hung.

Excited to show off the new interior design, I pounced on my husband when he returned home from work.

"Can't wait for you to see our new bedroom," I said, hands clasped over his eyes, walking him to the room.

"Wow, that sure is bright," he said, spinning around. "Did I mention I don't like floral? And bright colors aren't my thing. Did you save the receipts?"

"I didn't know you wanted to be involved," I said, biting my nails.

"Well, um, I just know I hate floral."

Oh, is that so? Why'd ya wait until now to say so?

"Here's the thing," I said, placing my hand on both his shoulders. "Either you can come with me to Benjamin Moore, Home Depot, JOANN's, Carpet One, and Bed Bath & Beyond or you can tap out. Do nothing. Nada."

Take that Mr. Opinionated.

"I'm out."

And just like that, I decorated our house. Alone. Just the way I planned.

After all, I've heard that shopping at IKEA increases your chances of divorce by fourteen-percent. Oh sure, that Fjellse bed frame and Brimnes nightstand look good in the store, but try putting it together. By the last line of instructions, you'll be hurling insults at each other and sleeping in separate beds.

Twenty-seven years later, after watching all the DIY I could bear, I believed decorating was best left to the experts. No more handmade curtains, repainted furniture, or antique store finds for me.

And, God as my witness, my husband initiated the idea of redecorating our living room.

"I noticed you've been looking online for decorating ideas. If you want, get new furniture. We've had this stuff for a while."

Come again?

That was all it took to start the search for decorators. Laura Valance Designs came highly recommended by my besties. At our initial appointment, she examined my current furniture, measured rooms, snapped countless photos, and asked my opinion. As she whisked out the door, she said, "We'll be in touch."

Weeks later she returned with paint chips, diagrams, and color copies of furniture, carpet samples, and objects d'art. She left her portfolio on the end table for my review.

The next day my husband leafed through the diagrams and said, "What about my supersized Big Daddy recliner? Where's that going to go?"

"Laura said we don't have room for it. Plus, it's maroon, so 1980s."

After several one-on-one appointments, we pieced together the perfect room. I oohed and aahed as the items trickled in via FedEx.

Laura arranged each piece as meticulously as a museum curator. Green marble topped accent table, leather ottomans, and wingback chairs, plus Feng Shui to boot. I practically cried at its unveiling.

"What do you think?" asked Laura, standing back to survey her work. "You like it?"

I stared at the smooth, plump sofa cushions, perfectly cornered coasters, neatly arranged accent pillows, and plush area carpet.

I'm in love.

"It's so perfect. I feel like I should vet out my friends

before they sit on it."

Then in stormed my husband with his buddy, Chris, sweaty and dirty from eighteen holes of golf.

Chris plopped down on the corner unit, seized a beige and floral pillow then proceeded to manhandle and massage it behind his back. At the same time, my husband wedged a beer can between the bottom sofa cushions, used the coffee table as a footrest, and let out a slow fart.

I couldn't handle it. My new room destroyed right before my eyes.

"That's it. I can't take it. Get away from the pillows. And Chris, your wife called. She needs you home right away."

Next project, man cave. I think the garage will work nicely.

WHEN CHURCH PEOPLE KNOCK

When you're first married, on a typical weekend, you sleep until 10:00 AM, wake up, make coffee, and go back to sleep. Imagine my surprise when my husband violated our ritual and decided to answer the door.

When it comes to the doorbell, my husband's like Pavlov's dog. He can't stand to ignore it.

Ding dong.

"Leave it," I said, patting my hair. "They'll go away. Besides, I'm not decent."

He rushed to the door, slid to a stop in stocking feet, and pulled it open, bare chest and all.

Did you NOT hear a single word I said? Let me be more clear. If you answer the door, hell will rain down on you.

I peeked around the corner, my slovenly appearance blocked by his body. Two unknown people stood outside my front door. I could tell by their formal attire, the man wearing a blue blazer with a collared shirt, the woman in a long dress with kitten heels, that it was church people from the Church of I-Want-to-Ruin-Your-Sundays.

My husband yanked the door opened, his half-nakedness exposed, much to the delight of the neighbors, and welcomed the visitors into our living room.

"Stacey, come out," he shouted as I attempted to bolt upstairs. "Someone's here to see us."

That fool.

I crept forward, wearing Betty Boop pajamas and fuzzy slippers. They took a seat and introduced themselves as Sue and Ron. They launched into incredible details about their church; it's location, philosophy, yadda yadda. At one point, they asked, "You have any questions?"

My husband said, "What's the difference between the Catholic and Lutheran religions?"

Hey, what's the big idea asking such a loaded question? I'm out of here the first chance I get.

They responded with the enthusiasm of a kid chewing a twelve-hour jawbreaker with a sour candy center. "Back in 1571, Martin Luther…" and droned on and on, covering 445 years in three hours.

This is gonna take a while.

My husband had a history of asking leading questions of strangers, neighbors, and relatives. Once at Christmas, he asked my grandmother to tell him the story of her childhood. That led to a five-hour discussion. Even my grandfather skipped out.

"Mike, you're on your own," Grandpa said, bouncing off the sofa like he was on fire. "I'm getting rum punch. Will. Not. Be. Back."

About midway through our "conversation" with the church folks, my husband made a move to escape. You know what I mean; he placed his hands on the edge of the divan and tried to rise.

"Hey buddy," I hissed. "Sit back down. You opened the door."

Then right before they left, they paused and asked me, "Do you have any questions?"

"Do you mind calling first the next time?"

I am going to hell.

With that, they grabbed their pamphlets and scattered faster than ants at a church picnic.

GRAND THEFT AUTO

On an island off the coast of the North Atlantic, Ireland offered my husband and me a promise of relaxation, the opportunity to decompress and regroup after the hustle and bustle of everyday life. Suffering the winter blues, we sought soothing Celtic music, meandering streams, lush landscapes, and a slower pace to celebrate our fifth wedding anniversary.

We had no idea that their laid-back ways could get us arrested, or worse, thrown in the slammer.

After eleven hours, we landed at Dublin Airport. We hauled four-mismatched Samsonite bags to customer service. I rummaged through my large carry-on and smacked down our Alamo Car Rental paperwork on the counter. The desk attendant, "Margaret," as stated in bold font on her name tag, eyeballed us, tapped a few keys, and pushed a button on the screen.

"Go out de exit ter peck up yisser car," she said, pointing with an index finger, nails bitten to the quick. "See dat white buildin' in de corner?" Her heavy Irish accent, full of hard consonants, dropped "g's" and soft vowels, made it tricky to understand.

This cannot be English.

The two assistant managers on duty, Katie and Liam, according to their nameplates, glanced up as we entered the dinky building then resumed watching "Gilligan's Island" reruns. It flashed static-y across the black and white portable television situated on the corner of the laminate desk.

"Margaret said we should come here," I said, shuffling my feet. "This is where we get the keys, right?"

Wake up, people. We've got things to do.

"Let me see your documentation," said Katie, running her pointer finger down the forms with a frown, smacking gum. "Seems there's a bit of a problem."

Dum-de-dum-dum-dum.

She shuffled over to Liam, causing computer paper, Post-Its, and manila folders on the messy desk to scatter to the floor. They huddled for a few seconds then she pointed in our direction.

What the hell? Whispering together like we're common criminals or something.

"Here you go," she said, depositing the keys in Mike's hand, her freckled, porcelain face contorted with attitude.

She disappeared into the back office as Liam pulled in front with a brand-new Ford Escort. Thin shouldered, with a belt cinched tight around baggy jeans, he also disappeared into the back office as the automobile idled curbside.

About fifteen minutes later, my husband shrugged his shoulders and said, "I don't think they're coming back. Let's go." He loaded our extensive luggage into a trunk as small as my clutch purse and the rest in the rear seat.

We referenced our map from the travel agent and

hit the road for the Dingle Peninsula. After two hours, we parked in the gravel lot at our bed and breakfast, Milltown House. We spied our host as he peeked out the living room curtains. He met us at the door and sauntered down a few steps to our car.

"Cheers," he said in a deep brogue. "You must be the Gustafsons. I'm Ian."

"That's us," we said in unison, nodding our heads.

"I'll get your bags," Ian said, as he struggled to drag four massive bags up the staircase and into the foyer.

Mike rushed behind him. "Let me help."

"Do you have your dead uncle in there?" said Ian, mouth curled into a mischievous grin.

Ha, ha, funny man.

Later we changed for dinner then went downstairs to examine our new accommodations.

"Ian, can you recommend a place to eat?" Mike said.

"Try Flanagan's Pub down the street. Good food. Irish music every night."

We scooted down to Flanagan's where Colleen, a stout, serious redhead, asked, "What'll you have?"

"I'll take the chicken with the vegetable plate. Plus a pint of Harp," I said. "Sounds yummy."

Mike ordered the beef stew plus a Guinness.

Minutes later, with a kaboom, Colleen deposited a huge ceramic platter on our table. I feasted my eyes upon the vegetable platter: French fries, baked potatoes, mashed potatoes, and a sliver of broccoli. The starchy, oily smell knocked me back in my seat.

Wow, the Irish love their potatoes.

After listening to traditional Irish music for a few hours, we returned to our B&B, bloated and tipsy.

We traveled around the Emerald Isle for ten more

days. On our last day, we bid goodbye and returned to the Dublin airport.

At the Alamo office, like a propane explosion, Katie rushed us much the same as long-lost relatives.

No idea the Irish could move so fast.

She glanced over our shoulder at the Ford Escort and burst into song.

"Jesus, Mary, and Joseph," she shouted as she flailed her hands by her side. "The car's back. The car's back."

She opened the rental car office door and screamed, "Liam, come quick. The car's back."

He raced into the office and embraced his co-worker. They wrapped us in a group hug as well.

"What's happening?" I asked.

"Thought you guys stole the car. You left before we completed the paperwork."

"We assumed you were finished," I said, willing Mike with my eyes to say something. "Did you call the cops on us?"

"Are you crazy lady? We were prayin' it'd turn up. Didn't tell the boss either."

Fugitives in a foreign land.

In a jiffy, Margaret, the desk attendant from the Alamo airport office, burst inside and they huddled together, clapping each other on the back. I overhead phrases like, *Thank Jesus* and *Count yer blessin*.

"Think we should take off now?" I said to Mike, stepping closer to the doorway.

With their backs turned, we beelined for the airport. Time to get out of dodge before we were accused of pilfering petty cash, the housing crisis, or the Famine of 1845.

Yea, luck of the Irish.

Rock-a-Bye Baby

I never anticipated that the day my husband caught the flu would be the day I had the best sleep of my life.

Mike came down with the crud; gross wet sniffles, ear-splitting cough, and monster sneezes. As soon as his congested head hit the pillow, he reared out of bed, and let rip the biggest, yuckiest aha-aha-choo I've ever heard. Then he spit up a pile of phlegm into a wad of tissues and followed it with serious hacking. I've never been more terrified to be near another person.

Seriously? I'm supposed to sleep next to that?

"That's it," I said. "I'm out of here." I snatched my overstuffed pillow, eyeglasses, and paperback books, then pussyfooted to the guest room.

Grandma's room, complete with fresh linen, ample lighting, and best yet, minus the sick husband, offered the uninterrupted sleep I craved in a germ-free zone. Last time I chanced to sleep next to He-Who-Spreads-Germs, I ended up nursing a cold for two weeks. No thank you.

Wide-eyed after the sonic nasal explosion, my heart was racing. I fluffed up the pillows, rearranged the comforter, and positioned two bolsters behind my back.

Then I grabbed a new novel, *Difficult Husbands*, and snuggled deep within the 1800-thread-count flannel sheets. "Oh, this is perfect," I said to myself and began reading.

"Cough, sputter," the racket echoed from down the hallway. I tiptoed out of bed, closed the guest room door, and sighed, "That's better."

Now that the room was soundproofed, it was just Sue Grafton and me. I turned pages for an hour and sunk deeper into the novel, passing out with it open across my chest. At 4:00 AM I rolled out of bed for a potty break. It took a few minutes for me to recollect my location. I snatched the book again and finished to the end of the chapter.

Pure bliss. I could read as long as I liked and sleep like a baby to boot. No one demanded that I shut off the light. Or called for more tissues. Or asked me what time it was. Again.

For the next five days, I slumbered in the guest room, escaping the hacking cough. Around day two, due to the long uninterrupted hours spent reading, I added a water pitcher and goblet to the bedside table.

This mama's thirsty.

By day three, I purchased a one-cup Keurig coffee maker, coffee pods, Sweet'N Low, and scones.

At the end of the week, our guest room resembled a bed-and-breakfast, complete with TV, computer, space heater, and stocked minibar. As long as Amazon kept delivering, I was happy as a kid on snow cone day.

In the morning, I bumped into my husband cooking breakfast.

"I'm feeling much better," he mumbled. "See," he said taking a big nose-clearing snort to reiterate his robust recovery. "Come back to our bedroom."

What?! And ruin my perfect new set up? Think again, Sir Hacks-a-Lot.

"Uh, that's great honey," I said, clearing my throat. "But now I think I picked up a bit of your cold, runny nose and scratchy throat," I whined, massaging my neck for extra effect.

"You're kidding. I was looking forward to a movie and snuggling with you tonight."

"Me too. What a bummer," I said, suppressing a smile, grabbing my newest Amazon delivery off the kitchen counter, *Why Do Men Have Nipples? Hundreds of Questions You'd Only Ask a Doctor After Your Third Martini.* "Don't worry about me. I'll be fine in the guest bedroom. I'll try to read a little."

Darn it, I've earned this!

MIKE SAVES EUROPE

After a unanimous vote, Paris became the destination for our family's summer vacation. Both of our college-aged kids agreed for the first time on a non-beach location.

Who are these people?

"Let's go to a place with a little history. I want to learn something instead of just vegging out on the beach," said my son, pulling a wad of HubbaBubba out of his mouth and sticking it on his sister's leg.

"Why do you have to be so gross?" she yelled at Brock, flicking away the gum. "But I agree. Let's learn a little this vacay."

After landing at Charles de Gaulle Airport, we were anxious to catch a cab and take a nap at our hotel before venturing out to sightsee. First, we would explore the Iron Lady, the great symbol of France. The Eiffel Tower held a magic that's hard to describe. Each year she hosted over seven-million visitors. They must know a thing or two.

We arranged a guided tour, all the bells and whistles, to start our treasured vacation. We had a million questions to ask. As we waited for our guide to meet us at the prearranged site, our family separated.

"I'm going to search for a bathroom before the guide gets here," I said, spotting the Parisian version of the porta-potty, a fully automated unisex self-cleaning outdoor public toilet.

Ooh la la. Ain't we fancy?

After ten minutes, Ashley jogged up to the bathroom to find me still waiting in line.

"Can't believe you're still here," she said. "By the way, Dad just went to tell security he found a backpack."

"What?" I said, twisting my face. "Where was it?"

"Leaning on the leg of the Eifel Tower. He didn't touch it," she said. "We must get to the meeting spot in five minutes."

After using the bathroom, Ashley and I marched arm in arm through the swarm of tourists in search of my husband and son.

But all of a sudden, tourists started murmuring and shuffling backward. The local police or the Police Nationale, with serious faces, began to move the crowd back and erected yellow barricade tape.

"What do you think's going on?" I said to my daughter, trying to get a glimpse through the sea of black jackets and weaving heads.

Ashley looked at me with wide eyes and said, "Do you think this is about the backpack?"

Oh my gosh. I could see the headlines now. Americans Cause Trouble.

People were jockeying for position to find out what was happening. Rubberneckers twisted their heads right and left, like wheat waving in the wind.

"Don't mention this to anybody," I said to Ashley in a hushed tone. "We need to be sure it was Dad."

I scanned the crowd and spotted my husband and

son across the street. I shook my finger in his direction and mouthed, "Was that you?" He shrugged his shoulders and smiled.

This will be our family's story to share for years.

Within moments, the police cleared out the area under the Eifel Tower and continued to put up caution tape. I craned my neck around the crowd and spotted SWAT emblazoned in yellow across the back of blue jackets.

Holy cow, Batman!

The SWAT team positioned their bodies inside the caution tape and cordoned off the area to get their van through. A black, compact surveillance robot, about the size of a medium suitcase, with a mobile arm anchored on top, was released from the back of the van and rolled toward the backpack. At that point, the large crowd and angle of the street blocked my view.

Kapow! We heard explosions near the robot.

"What was that?" my daughter said, wrinkling her brow.

"The robot probably used an explosive to blow up the backpack."

After a time, the police allowed visitors back in the area. It wasn't too difficult to locate our family since we're all tall like giraffes.

I rushed over and hugged my husband and whispered, "Gosh that was scary. Do you think that was because of the backpack you found?"

"Definitely. From where we were standing I could see the whole thing."

"Well guys it is official," I said, turning to my kids. "Your dad's a hero. He saved the Eifel Tower, he saved Paris, you could even say he saved Europe," I said, beaming at Mike.

Then my son chimed in, "Or you could say Dad ruined the vacation of 10,000 people."

Moment over.

ASLEEP AT THE WHEEL

To some, a car trip is an opportunity to see the nation, spend time with family, or play stupid car games like spot that license plate. But for me it's a chance to take a nap. By the time the bags are loaded, seat belts buckled, and the car backed down the driveway, I'm comatose. I just can't help it.

My husband and I shared driving responsibilities when we dated in college. That ended the day I offered to drive five hours from Rock Island, Illinois to St. Louis, Missouri.

Lost and sleepy in the Midwest.

It all went down pretty fast. We blasted out of his parents' place after a weekend visit. Right before we pulled away, Mike said, "I have a huge final tomorrow morning. Think you can drive us home?"

"Does a one-legged duck swim in a circle?" I said, circling around to hop in the driver's side.

Knowing my propensity to snooze in the car, he added, "Here, take one of these to stay awake," and tossed me a Coke. "I'll guide you to the on-ramp, then it's pretty much straight all the way."

Despite the caffeine, about one hour into the trip I

must have blacked out. I may have been awake physically, but mentally checked out somewhere between Rock Island and Chicago.

Honestly, I shut my eyes for a second and *whoosh*.

Mike had focused on his homework the instant we were on the straightaway. After three hours, he peered up from his textbook, face contorted, eyes narrowed and said, "Where are we?"

"Not sure but we've made good time."

"Think we better pull over and check," he said.

Remember pre-GPS days?

Inside an Exxon gas station, he stared at the map on the wall and mumbled something like *What the hell! Chicago?* He begged me to switch seats.

That's right folks. Instead of driving due south, I drove east and landed us about forty minutes from Chicago. In other words, we ended up two and a half hours out of our way.

When we first married, a typical car trip involved a quick run to the beach. By the time we approached the highway entrance, my thoughts usually wandered and yawning commenced.

Can't wait to feel the hot sand on my body. So warm. So soft.

"Want to stop in Santa Cruz?" my husband asked, poking me in the side.

"Waaa? You talking to me?" I dabbed my drool with a tissue.

"For God's sake, keep it together. We've only been gone an hour."

Our weekend jaunts ended once we had two kids and car trips involved more than just packing a beach bag on the fly. But when they reached their teens, we ventured out again, braving treks to San Diego over Christmas break when the weather was chilly in the evening and perfect during the day. I volunteered to ride shotgun because I knew trips were boring for the driver and it was hard to stay alert and navigate.

"Let me help this trip," I said giving his hand a squeeze. "I'll be your co-pilot."

He said, "Are you up for the responsibility?"

"What do you mean?"

"Rip Van Winkle, stay awake."

How hard can that be?

Throughout the drive, I doled out sunflower seeds by the handful and replaced the highly caffeinated Mountain Dew the moment he slurped it down.

"Hey, Ashley, throw the snacks up here," I said to my fifteen-year-old daughter, hands outstretched.

I ripped open the yellow bag and scooped out a handful of Funyuns.

"Open wide," I said. I stuffed the crunchy, oniony treat into his mouth.

In addition to feeding him junky snacks, I controlled the music selection and volume or screamed the occasional, "Oh my God. Watch out for that semi!"

But soon I rubbed my eyes and leaned back for a little shuteye. Just a few minutes of zz's and I'd be fresh.

Shotgun duties make Mommy tired.

"Hey, wake up," he said, glancing over and nudging me in the ribs. "You promised to keep awake."

"Settle down. I'm awake."

In retribution, he rolled down the windows and blasted us with arctic air and Van Halen. As an additional reminder, he tapped on the brakes. My head wobbled back and forth.

Not funny, dude!

About seven hours in, the car drifted into another lane. I felt a subtle adjustment but nodded back down for forty winks. Neither honking nor the threat of impending disaster could keep my eyes open.

Car seats are comfy, like tiny cocoons. Combined with an efficient heater, reclining seats, and gentle rocking, I'm out faster than Grandpa in an easy chair.

"Dad!" Ashley said from the backseat, voice filled with panic. "Wake up!"

I spun around out of a perfectly peaceful repose.

What's a gal got to do to get some shuteye around here?

"That's it," she said, throwing her hands in the air. "Mom, I'm riding in the front so I can see Dad's eyes. You get in back."

My plan worked perfectly. *Hasta la vista* front seat. I curled up in the back with a neck wrap, snuggie, and the snack bag. I'm fine in the back.

Ashley's shotgun duties received a five-star rating on Yelp.

You want to ride shotgun? Have at it.

TWO THUMBS UP

Hitchhiking today is as popular as a middle seat on United Airlines. Back in the day, people could stick out a thumb or hold up a cardboard sign with, "Daytona Beach or Bust" scrawled in Magic Marker and hop in the next car for a free ride. Then along came movies like *The Texas Chain Saw Massacre* and ruined it for everyone. Now we fear a psychopathic hitchhiker resides behind every thumb.

Ten years after college graduation, I planned a rendezvous with my best friend, Lynne and her husband, Dave. Since they lived in New York and we resided in Colorado, coordination took months to work out. After mulling over possibilities, we agreed on Ireland, the Emerald Isle. Our pressure-filled jobs and long hours lured us to her craggy shores with the promise of a slower pace.

We arranged a meet up at Murphy's, a popular bar in Killarney, about fifty miles from the Shannon Airport.

"Oh my gosh," I said as I hurried over to give Lynne and Dave a big hug, knocking down a barstool on my way. "So happy to see you."

We toasted with cold brews, light beer for the gals

and dark ale, Guinness, for the guys.

"Isn't this amazing," I said, with a slow, disbelieving shake of my head. "Can't believe after five years we reunite in Ireland."

The next day we jumped into our separate cars to explore the west coast, specifically the Cliffs of Moher. You see, the vehicles there are tiny. Imagine the smallest car you know and insert the word mini. Not all our luggage fit in the trunk so we had to stick the extras in the back seat.

Our drive to the Cliffs stretched for five miles. At times, we were amazed that our vehicles didn't go careening off the edge of the highway or clip someone hitching on the side of the road.

"Hey," I said with a tilt of my head out the car window. "There's another one."

In Ireland, it seemed like everybody hitched a ride, from older women to sulking teenage boys and scruffy college kids. I pointed out the fifth hitchhiker spotted that day. He lazily stuck his thumb out hoping to catch a ride. He positioned his oversized khaki backpack and black canvas duffle at his feet as he casually attempted to give travelers' eye contact.

As we zoomed by, I said to my husband, "Man, lots of hitchhikers in Ireland."

"Yeah, it's a great way to get around," he said eyes brightening. "Here it's easy to get a lift from one village to another. Technically, it's illegal on the highway but the police won't bother you."

"Interesting."

"Want to pick one up?"

An axe-wielding murderer? No thanks.

"Oh god no," I said with a quick, high-pitched laugh.

"I'd be too scared."

"Nothing to be afraid of," he said with a grin. "Did I ever tell you the story about when my brother and I hitchhiked?"

In the 1980s, for three weeks my husband hitched it across Ireland with his brother, Brian, as their primary mode of transportation.

"We used our lawn-mowing money to go after graduation," he said, tapping the steering wheel to the beat of *Uptown Funk*.

Keep in mind, this was pre-GPS. Maps only. No cell phones.

"We discovered that six-foot-three-inch young men traveling with large backpacks and small suitcases don't easily fit into small cars," he said cocking his head to the side. "Not everyone was thrilled to offer us a ride."

Nonetheless, many brave souls allowed them into their personal space even when they were moldy from walking in the Irish rain. The Irish claim eleven levels of rain from spitting and wetting rain to lashing and hammering. The boys trudged through it all until a kind local picked them up.

"One time we were nearly plowed down by a guy coming around the corner in the middle of bucketing rain. Shrubs blocked visibility. Turns out he was the son of the guy we had arrangements to meet up with in Turles, Michael Burke."

"Wow, what a coincidence," I said.

"You get picked up, you swap stories, and for the moment you're friends. The Irish have an amazing gift of gab."

After he finished reminiscing, we spotted a young brown-haired guy and his fair-haired girlfriend at the side of the road, thumbs up.

"I think it's time I pay it forward," he said easing to the side of the road." Let's give them a lift."

What's happening?

"Need a ride?" Mike yelled out the window.

Lynne and Dave pulled off the road behind us and waited in their car.

The couple spoke to each other privately and then the young man said in broken English, "Which way you going?"

"Off to Kilkenny Castle," Mike said, pointing north.

They conferred with each other for a moment and then nodded in agreement.

"This works best if you guys come in our car and put your luggage in our friend's car," he said, gesturing with his elbow at Lynne and Dave's car.

They whispered some more in French then tentatively entered our vehicle and kept an eye out as their backpacks were loaded into the boot of our friend's car.

Chill, we have enough luggage of our own.

"Parlez-vous français?" Mike said, using his limited French.

At the castle, tours were offered in many languages, including French. We could tell by their hesitation that their budget was limited.

"We'd like to pay your admission," Mike told them.

"Thanks," they said.

At the conclusion of the tour, the six of us met outside the castle.

"What direction you going?" the Frenchman asked.

Our next destination did not meet their plans and we parted ways, but not before they gave us hugs and a note with their address and an offer to visit.

On the way to the next leg of our journey, we spied yet another hitchhiker.

"Want to give her a ride?" my husband said, pointing to an older woman by the side of the road wearing a ratty jacket and carrying multiple bags.

We edged the vehicle to the side. As she ran to our car, we realized it was a man, not an older lady. With a deranged look, his jacket flapping and trash flying out the bags, he raced forward.

"Put the pedal to the metal. Let's go," I said.

Hitchhiking may be a way to meet interesting people like a priest, international students, and a barkeep, but for me, psycho killers still lurk around every corner.

MONEY TALKS

My husband's always nagging me, "We need to discuss our finances." For me, this topic was about as exciting as Gwyneth Paltrow talking about a Himalayan smoothie and her non-toxic, organic skincare line.

Just stop.

Saturday morning, I skidded into the room wearing my slipper socks and spied my husband parked on the sofa.

Perched on the edge of our sectional, surrounded by stacks of yellow notepads, loose-leaf paper, spiral notebooks and four pens neatly arranged at a right angle on the edge of the coffee table, he looked open for business. My heart raced.

"Glad you're up," he said maintaining strong eye contact and a thin smile. "I've saved you a seat."

It's a trick.

"Do you have a few minutes to talk about our finances?"

Quick. Think. Must find a way to get out of this.

"Umm, I have an appointment in five minutes."

Don't look him in the eye.

"Come on," he said, patting a spot next to him. "It's

the weekend."

For the last few months, he's been hounding me to review over twenty-five years worth of our finances.

Look Buddy, I'll keep doing the laundry and making dinner if you keep doing all that money stuff.

"Seriously, this is important," he said, scraping his hair back. "You need to understand our finances. Do you even remember how to access our banking information? What would you do if I wasn't around?"

"I'd call your best friend, Jeff. He probably knows the passwords to our bank account."

"What?!?"

"Just kidding. Fine. You have my attention."

For the next three minutes.

He shoved a pen and pad of paper into my hand.

"Might want to take a few notes."

Not going to happen. Must act dumb.

I managed to stay awake as my husband droned on and on about budgets, long-term versus short-term investments, financial portfolios, goals, emergency funds, dividends, blah, blah, blah, and taxes.

Lost me at notes.

"Let's begin by discussing the college fund," he said waving his arms.

We still have kids in college?

I glanced at my watch. Only ten minutes had passed since I sat down but it felt like an eternity. He pulled out the laptop and balanced it on his knees. Using a pencil as a pointer, he flashed up on the screen charts bearing all types of data. My eyes blurred under the strain of bar, pie, and line charts.

My man came to this battle prepared.

"What level of risk are we willing to take with the

529 Plan? Do you think a market risk is best?"

"Oh...um...sure. I agree," I said, nodding like a bobble-headed dashboard dog. "You are so smart."

What the hell's he talking about? Did he say whisk? Or was it disk? Bisque?

"Do you think you can start looking into the difference between capital gains and dividend income on an annual basis for some of our investments?"

Is he still talking to me?? Hey Buddy, as soon as you figure out the steam setting on the dryer, I'll start helping with the finances.

After forty-seven minutes, I slumped over the sofa arm and pretended to hang myself. I wrapped an imaginary rope around my neck and stuck out my tongue for emphasis.

"Seriously?" he said in a whinny voice. "I lost you all ready? This is important."

"Do you really think I can go from doing nothing to making major decisions about our finances?" I said.

"I believe in you. I know you're capable of helping."

"Won't it all work itself out in the long run anyway?"

"What the heck are you talking about?" he said through gritted teeth.

"Or how about this?" I said touching his arm. "I'll take baby steps and begin by collecting our yearly expenses."

"That sounds good. Let's follow up on this next month."

Come again? Next month?

Mouth slack, he slithered away, shaking his head and mumbling something like, "*God help us.*"

Whoosh, thunk, thump, thumk.

The low hum of the dryer and the muted thumping

of tumbling clothes resounded from the laundry room.

My husband swaggered into the living room with a puffed-up chest and a *Well?* attitude.

"Fine," I said, sighing dejectedly. "You win."

Unfortunately, my husband likes a challenge, so now my shirts are wrinkle free and I'm learning about itemized deductions.

HOTLIPS HOULIHAN AND THE NEEDY PATIENT

"You'll be off your foot for four to six weeks," the young doctor said to Mike with a no-nonsense attitude, glancing my way for emphasis. "Absolutely no weight bearing activity."

What?! Wait?! Who's going to barbeque? Take out the trash cans? Carry laundry up the steps? Kill bugs?

"Any questions?" Doctor Doogie asked arms crossed, staring at my husband's optimistic face.

"Do you think I'll be able to play in a golf tournament in August?" he asked half-joking.

Are you insane? You'll be lucky to drive a golf cart in ten weeks.

Last Friday, Mike arrived back home around midnight after bonding with my son at fraternity Father/Son Weekend.

"Holy cow, what happened?" I said, sucking in a quick breath as my husband hopped in from the garage, dragging his left leg.

"I think I tore something," he said, wincing with every step. "I heard a pop and a snap diving for the dice."

"What were you playing?"

"Beer die," he explained with a smirk. "Father-Son teams. One team throws a die into the air and the other team catches it before it flies off of the table."

Not exactly NFL football.

"I'll be fine," he said.

But he wasn't. He tossed and turned all night. In the morning, he smothered his leg with ice packs and tried to ride it out.

By Tuesday, the pain became unbearable and he hauled butt to the doctor. Official diagnosis, fully ruptured Achilles tendon.

A quick Google search confirmed our worst fears. Surgery was inevitable and a return to his former level of activity would take up to six months. Any hopes of playing the senior basketball league, dashed.

LeBron, you'll have to forget about that rematch.

Outpatient surgery lasted two hours and he left groggy plus crutches. Once home, I helped him through the front door into the den, his temporary home.

"Honey, lie down," I said, patting a place on the sofa. The den looked like a hospital room with pillows, blankets, and slippers to boot. "I set up a TV tray for the remote, water glass, reading glasses, magazines, and books. If you need anything, I'll be right here."

He elevated his leg with a giant pillow, covered up with a blanket, snatched the remote, and slept for the next four hours. His movement was limited to the sofa and occasional trips to the bathroom.

By the second day, I realized my workload had more than doubled. Plus, he shot out requests faster than an auctioneer on *Storage Wars*.

Glancing up from his iPhone, he said, "Can you get

me the pain meds?"

Hey, a little eye contact here.

"Sure."

"Do you mind bringing me a glass of water?" he said, shaking the water bottle my way.

Geez, I brought him water yesterday! And what's with the shaking?

"I need fresh ice," he said as he pointed to the huge machine that pulsed cold water through the hoses in his leg wraps to control inflammation.

"Where are my crutches?" "Do we have any snacks?" "What's for dinner?" "Can you scratch my pinky toe?" The demands never ceased.

On day five, the seriousness of his injury began to sink in. My man would be out all summer and I would pay the price. He was unable to do even the most minuscule tasks like put a plate in the dishwasher, let the dog out, or answer the phone.

For days, I methodically refilled twenty pounds of ice into the machine. And made three squares a day. And cleaned up the mess.

By day nine, I felt like Hotlips Houlihan, the nurse in the television series M*A*S*H, and I wanted a transfer.

My mother called to check on the infirm. "How's Mike?"

"Better each day," I said through a clenched jaw. "But I'm exhausted."

"Sorry honey," she said. "Are you still coming for a visit next month?"

"Doubtful. Have to play it by ear."

It was impossible to fathom bringing crutches, a knee scooter, ice machine, carry-on, and checked luggage through the airport, much less trying to rent a car. The odds of Mike getting reinjured were not worth the risk.

Fortunately, by week two, he stopped the painkillers and hopped around on one foot.

"I decided to go back to work on Monday," he announced, grinning like Jim Carrey in *Ace Ventura*.

Work? If he can get to work, he can get a damn glass of water.

He'd been sleeping in the guest bedroom because of his colossal walking boot and the multiple pillows needed to elevate it.

"I'm going to try to sleep in the master bedroom tomorrow," he said as I kissed him good night.

"Are you sure you're ready for it?" I said with trembling hands. "Our bed's six inches higher and harder to maneuver. Maybe you should play it safe and wait a little longer."

Damn, my days of hogging the whole bed were over.

By week five, I started to avoid him. Tink, thunk, tink, thunk. The sound of crutches across the floor, followed by the heavy drag of a walking boot, sent shivers. It meant he was nearby and needed a "favor."

My mother called to check in again. "How's our patient?"

"He's in less pain, but still off his foot," I said with a yawn.

"Why don't you come home alone? Get a little R&R. He'll be fine. I'll make your favorites, toasted ravioli and Italian chopped salad."

"Will you make your famous gooey butter cake too? Massage my feet?"

"Anything you want."

"How's your schedule look for next Friday?"

One-way non-stop flight to St. Louis. Mama didn't raise no fool.

BRAIN FARTS

I bet your husband's like mine and doesn't remember anyone's name. From church folks to relatives, his transgressions are too numerous to count.

Mike swears he never forgets a face, but names? That's an entirely different issue. Sitting in the bleachers during our high school daughter's varsity basketball game, he engaged in an animated discussion with another dad. Both daughters had played on the same team since fifth grade. For years, we've celebrated wins and mourned losses over margaritas and chips. The parents have even been to our home on holidays.

Side by side on the bleachers, for an hour, the guys discussed everything from the latest NBA scandal and their colleagues in the industry, to the best craft beer.

"Definitely Three Floyds Dark Lord," Mike said, waving his hands for emphasis. "Got to get out to Munster, Indiana sometime to taste their brew."

"Well, looks like our girls take the win," his buddy said with a glance at the team high-fiving each other. "See you next Thursday."

"Great talking to you, Dave," Mike said, giving him a fist pump.

"It's Jim," he said rolling his eyes.

Mike watched as Jim eased down ten rows of bleachers, shaking his head, and never looking back.

"Well, that was embarrassing," I said, scooching closer to his side.

Brain fart.

My man's mind is mush when it comes to friends' names, but ask him to recite a work email from ten years ago, and he doesn't miss a beat.

His memory lapses didn't end on the court either.

One time at church, Mike tapped a parishioner on the shoulder and proceeded to converse with him between the sign of peace and communion.

"Going deer hunting again this year?" he said, leaning an elbow on the pew in front of us.

"Um…maybe. Haven't really given it much thought," the man said, eyebrows squished together.

"By the way, I bumped into your mom at the grocery store last weekend. She's so excited to have a new grandbaby soon."

"Hmmm…okay," he said turning around to stuff his face in the hymnal.

After services ended, Mike made a big display of giving him a one-arm man hug and said, "Have a good one."

We scooted past the pastor in the recessional line. At our parked car I asked Mike, "By the way, who do you think you were talking to?"

"Rob," he said with a *duh* expression. "Laura's husband."

"Nope. But I will grant you this, they look vaguely similar. That's John, Cindy's ex-husband."

"Seriously?" he said but his face conveyed *I don't think so.*

"Lucky for you they're both hunters."

His memory lapses didn't end at church. On Saturday morning, we snuggled in down blankets and prepared to binge watch *Scandal* for several hours.

"Someone's at the door," I said. Stanley, our long-haired cock-a-chon, wagged his tail back and forth in agreement. "Can you get it?" I asked my husband. With an old man groan, Mike pushed off the sofa and rushed to the front door.

I heard a familiar voice and peeked down the hallway. On our front porch stood Sheila, my cousin, holding two Starbucks cups and an aluminum pan.

"Hey…. you…come on in," my husband stuttered and flagged me by his side.

"Thanks," she said with a smile. She wore black Nike sweats with coordinated sneakers. She twisted a tendril of brown hair and said, "Just happened to be in the neighborhood. Brought you some brownies."

"How's the big guy and the little one?" Mike blurted, scratching his neck. Sheila gave a slight headshake and crossed the threshold into the foyer.

Classic.

We gossiped together for about an hour. "Got to pick up Jimmy from soccer," she said as she hopped off the recliner. She snatched car keys from the end table and left.

Once she departed, I frowned at Mike. "You didn't remember her name, did you?"

"Yes I did," Mike said, cracking his knuckles.

"Then what is it?"

This is going to be good.

"Cindy? Sandy? Suzy?" he asked as I shook my head.

"Nice try. That was Sheila," I said rubbing the back

of my neck. "How come you can't remember any of my relatives' names? You know Ragave's name, the owner of the Indian Restaurant."

"Maybe that's because Cindy, Sandy, Suzy has never made me Tandoori Chicken," he said as he wiped his brow and strutted away.

Knock knock.

Stanley yapped at the door to greet our latest guest. Through the peephole, I spied Ed, our next-door neighbor.

Mike yanked it open. "Hey Ed, what's going on?"

He traipsed in, lugging a jumbo crock-pot and a medium-sized Tupperware container.

"The wife asked me to return this," he said as he passed it over to Mike. "And give you some of the best chili I've ever eaten."

"No problem. Looks delicious. Want to come in for a beer?"

"Can't," he said giving Mike a high five. "Got errands to run. See you later Brian. Bye Stacey."

Awkward.

"Can you believe it?" Mike said sagging against the front door. "Ed forgot my name. Been neighbors for twenty years."

Who'd a thunk it?

SHAKE YOUR BOOTY

When first married, I rummaged through catalogs for hours, dog-earing pages of gift ideas for my husband's birthday from watches to dress-shirts and beyond. For anniversaries, nothing substituted traditional presents, like paper for the first anniversary or cotton for the second. It seemed appropriate to stop at the tenth, tin and aluminum. Really?

Quite frankly, I'm stumped when it comes to buying a gift for Mike, and he's no help. After avoiding the malls the entire year, he routinely shops for clothes a week before the holidays. What?!? Why?

If it's too expensive, he'll return it. If he really wanted it, he's already bought it. Whiskey glasses? Meat of the Month Club? Make Your Own Hot Sauce Kit? Deep sea sand art?

What do you want??

"Have you given any thought to what you'd like for Christmas?" I asked Mike, leaning in closer to make sure he maintained eye contact. My man's attention span is shorter than a military haircut.

"Oh, nothing," he said with a shrug.

"Come on," I said tapping my fingers on the table.

"There must be a gadget you'd like."

"Your love is all I need," he said, laying a hand over his heart.

That's sweet. Now tell me what you want!

A mini-portable sleep machine screamed, "pick me" from a top shelf at CVS.

According to the box, *SoundSpa* played soothing all-natural sounds, as indicated on the dial by soothing names such as white noise, tranquil, relax, peace, and calm. The manufacturer stated, "It's meant to cover up the noises that could keep you awake."

I got some of those.

To operate the sound machine, press the timer button to indicate the minutes desired by toggling through thirty, sixty, ninety minutes or overnight. It even sported a loop with a timer.

On Christmas Day, he unwrapped the festooned box, said, "Thanks," and promptly stowed it away in the nearest drawer. *Poof.* That was that.

Bon voyage, SoundSpa. Off to the trash you go.

At bedtime, the unexpected happened.

"Do you know if we have a spare outlet?" he said, ransacking our bedroom. He pushed aside the end table and kicked around a pile of dirty laundry.

Chill out. It's not that great.

He found an outlet, set the dial to ocean, and snuggled into the down comforter. A smile emerged on his face.

For months, he'd been complaining about my snoring. Like he had a lot of room to talk. I'd endured his snorts and wheezes for the last twenty-six years.

I brushed my teeth as gentle ocean waves beckoned me to our boudoir. But after thirty minutes in bed, I tossed and turned. Then it stopped.

What?! Set for thirty minutes? Come on!

In the morning, I rubbed my neck and asked Mike, "How'd you sleep?"

"Best ever," he said bouncing out of bed with bright shiny eyes. "Head hit the pillow and kaboom. Love it."

"Well, I missed out," I said clenching my jaw. "Thirty minutes is not long enough."

Day two, he pressed the power button, tucked the blanket under his chin, and was out.

But bedside, our sweet little twenty-pound pup, Stanley, huddled closer and tried to leap into my arms.

"Hey little guy," I said stroking his fluffy head. "What going on?"

He shook like a Vegas showgirl, and his eyes pleaded, *help me.*

"Hey," I said, poking my husband in the ribs. "Something's wrong with Stanley."

"Zzzzzzzz."

When I deposited him back into the dog bed, he scratched at the door and darted out of the room.

In the morning, I discovered him shaking by the side of the bed.

"You okay?" I said, scratching his belly and scooping him up.

I called Dr. Claws, our vet, and she said in a no-questions-asked way, "Bring him in."

"I think Stanley's having a seizure," I said in the examination room.

Her severe black haircut and piercing eyes snapped me to attention. Stanley showed his displeasure by fidgeting as she weighed and checked his temperature.

She scares me too.

After looking into his eyes, ears, and mouth, she said with hand on hip, "Has anything changed in your household?"

Wait a second.

"Yep, we bought a sound machine," I said.

"What's that?"

"You know, it plays white noise to help you get to sleep."

"That's it. Your dog's trying to tell you, 'Get that shit out of here.' In five days, he should be better. If not, come back."

She scooted away and pointed to the door. I spied a sign on the side of the desk, "Your pets will love us. We Shih Tzu not."

I think not.

"How'd it go at the vet?" my hubby said when we returned.

"The sound machine's got to go," I announced. "Dr. Claws said it's giving Stanley severe anxiety."

"You're kidding," he said, face all melty-looking and shoulders stooped. "I need my white noise."

Guess my snoring will have to do.

Suffice it to say, after twenty-seven years, we've now reached the gift-card-giving stage of marriage. Or cash. Cash is good.

PARENTS

"My parents are getting older and I worry more. Now when they don't answer the phone, I figure they're either watching Wheel of Fortune, at Cracker Barrel, or dead."

—Stacey Gustafson, Sanctuary Ultra Lounge, Livermore, CA

Bingo Ain't for Sissies

"What do you want to do tonight?" I asked my mother as I tilted my head to the side. We go through this routine every time I visit. Finding an activity that didn't involve eating was as difficult as the temptation challenge on the *Biggest Loser*.

"Well, how 'bout bowling?" my mom asked, pushing her eyeglasses up on her nose.

"Nah, too boring. Any other ideas?"

"Want to play miniature golf?"

No way. I can never get my ball past that stupid windmill.

"Too hard."

"How about Bingo? Tuesday's my regular night. I'll introduce you to all my friends."

Visions of senior citizens, bratwurst, and daubers danced in my head.

At the local American Legion Hall, florescent lights hovered overhead. A low hum lingered in the air as the crowd lined up to purchase their Bingo cards and instruction sheet. Over 200 players, ranging in ages from forty to ninety, jockeyed for their turn at the cash box. I chucked down $12 for nine Bingo cards.

Nine cards?! This may be more difficult than it seems.

People hustled to their seats bearing bulging bags of Bingo supplies like chair cushions, snacks, and daubers in neon colors.

At our table, my mother and her boyfriend, Buddy, arranged their lucky charms around the Bingo sheets. A rabbit's foot, four-leaf clover keychain, troll dolls, pictures of my kids, and an elephant with trunk up encircled the table.

I plopped down in a seat nearby bearing only my purse and an open-minded attitude.

"Sorry young lady, that's Thelma's lucky seat," a woman said, pointing to her chest. On the metal table, she slammed down a stack of Bingo sheets, a two-liter bottle of Mountain Dew, and a picture of two young kids, most likely her grandchildren.

"Oh, sorry," I said, scooching over one more place.

I ain't no dummy. I've heard about grandmothers banned for life by their Bingo club after a fight over a "lucky chair."

Thelma proceeded to hog the rest of the table plus the one next to it with over thirty sheets.

How can she keep track of all these sheets? A regular Rainman.

"Want some pull-tabs?" Buddy asked, wearing his lucky t-shirt that said, *"Do me a favor and stop talking."*

He doled out $1 pull-tabs, multi-layered paper tickets containing symbols hidden behind perforated tabs, a little side game to add to the Bingo excitement.

How have I been missing out on this all these years?

After folks settled into their favorite seats, the music stopped and Mike, the Bingo caller, clutched the microphone and yelled, "Folks let's get started. Turn off your cell phones. Tonight's first Bingo is a Red Special."

White ping-pong balls imprinted with letters and numbers rotated around and around in a wire cage. He plucked them out one at a time.

"B12…N32…G57…"

And away he went. The pace was as fast as a college statistics class. I leaned over to my mother and said, "What was that last call?"

"Shhhhhhhhh," said the rest of the room.

Excuuuuse me!

I struggled to keep up.

Got to go to the John. Don't old people have to go all the time?

Suddenly Mike held up his hand for quiet. "I've been accused of cheating," he said, emphasizing his message with a fist pound. "Been a Bingo caller for thirty years. No way to cheat."

Then his wife, Betty, yelled out, "My husband's no cheater."

Soon Mike resumed calling the game. Then I noticed people shuffled in their seats. The sound of sheets being torn off of the Bingo pad resounded around the room.

"Mom, why's everyone wiggling around?" I asked.

"Someone's getting ready to call BINGO," my mother said, twisting her face in irritation.

Sure enough, over my right shoulder, a woman sporting oversized eyeglasses and a sequined tank top waved a yellow-lighted wand and yelled, "BINGO."

"Bring that Bingo to the front," Mike said, pointing to a volunteer. "Need to verify." Peering down his lenses, he hollered, "Not a good Bingo," and continued calling the numbers.

A huge sigh rippled across the room. A few muttered "shit" and "damn." You better be sure you have an actual

BINGO before you yell it out.

Soon an elderly gentleman wearing a fedora yelled, "Bingo," and a volunteer rushed over to confirm it.

He gave the thumbs up sign to Mike who announced, "Good Bingo."

The winner snapped up $35, and the next game started. Two hours and eight more games later, Bingo ended.

After three hours, a charley horse cramped my thigh, and I had to hold on to a chair to steady myself. Perspiration gathered on my upper lip, and my armpits stank like a rugby player.

We trashed the papers, rounded up our supplies, and waved our goodbyes.

"Nice meeting you Thelma, Mike, Bernice, Lucille…," I said and scurried toward the exit.

Bingo ain't for sissies. It's like miniature golf on steroids. Consider yourself lucky if you get out of there without a back injury or a black eye.

ALEXA, TURN ON THE OVEN

I'll hand it to my mother. She never gives up trying to keep up with new technology. This year I decided it was my responsibility to break her into the 21st century, one new gadget at a time. After all, she's the woman who taught me to eat with a spoon, tie my shoes, and love the King of Rock and Roll.

On her birthday, I handed her a floral wrapped box. "Mom, enjoy your new digital camera," I said. "You can send pictures through email or print them out at home."

"What's email?"

This is going to take awhile.

I instructed her how to get started. She opened the box, pulled out the camera, and then promptly handed it to my husband, Mike.

"Can you take the pictures, please?" she said, batting her eyelashes, dangling the camera strap with her outstretched hand towards his face.

"Mom, come on. It's easy," I said from the other side of the room. "Give it a try."

"Mike's so much better at taking pictures," she whined.

And a few years ago, we sent her our old laptop.

"How's the computer going?" I asked months later.

"Oh, I'm afraid to get started," she said, a slight tremor in her voice. "Don't want to break it."

"You can't do any damage. Just give it a shot."

Since I lived out of town and was only able to offer limited help through the phone, she found a computer tutor at the senior center, one who answered all her irrelevant and confusing questions. Soon I received emails that said, "Did you get this?"

No, I did not.

I encouraged her to add a cheap printer to her new "office," but she was satisfied with her system of begging me to send hard copies via snail mail.

During my visit back to the Midwest, she handed me a Christmas list full of surprises.

"What's this you want?" I said, confused by the page ripped from a Target ad.

"An Alexa. Maybe she can help me around the house."

This from the same woman who turns off her cell phone to save battery power after leaving me a voice message? From the airport.

Alexa, a device that uses voice commands to control your whole house, was too futuristic for my mother.

To clarify, I asked her, "What do you want Alexa to do?"

"Turn on the oven. Play music. Order a pizza."

"What, you think you just say 'Alexa, turn on the oven?'"

"Kind of."

"It doesn't work like that. You need a smart home."

"I'm getting sick of you calling me stupid."

"Mom, Alexa doesn't support appliances like yours, built before 1970."

"That's probably all my stuff," she said, looking around the room. "Can it at least adjust the heat with a voice command?"

"You'd have to retrofit smart products into your home. Well, maybe I can help you stream music from Spotify," I said.

"What's that?" she asked.

"It's the best way to listen to music on mobile or tablet."

"What's a tablet?"

"Never mind. Let's just focus on your laptop," I said. "Do you have a wireless network set up?"

"I don't know."

I shouldn't have even asked.

I knew better than to use actual equipment terms. Throwing around fancy words like wireless and network was a rookie move. These are my parents I'm talking about. They routinely say things like, "Did you see the story about the pandas on The Intranet."

"Where's the box with the wires hanging out?" I asked.

"Oh, that thing that AT&T installed? It's in the guest room. Behind the table. Under a blanket."

After spying her equipment, I asked, "What's your password?"

"Hold on. Let me find my notes." And she began flipping through a stack of Post-It notes five inches thick.

"It's either JoanChickadee or Grandma8675," she said, eyes pinched. "Wait, try BananaMama."

WTH! That's a pretty big swing.

We usually go through this game several times a week. I ask her to write it down, and she calls the following week with the same request. "Do you know my password?" I know the experts warn against writing down passwords, but there's only so much I can take. We settled on changing her password to "ForGodsSake."

About this time, I called Mike from her landline, an avocado wall-mounted phone that looked vaguely similar to the one I had in high school, kinked cord and all.

My hubby's patience and technical savvy was legendary. If he couldn't figure out how to solve her technical difficulties, no one could.

She sat wide-eyed near the telephone, focused on every word my husband said. She twisted her face a couple of times in confusion.

After an hour, Mom plopped in the chair and handed me the phone.

"Please tell your mother I changed my number," he said right before he disconnected.

My mother broke my husband.

ONE WOMAN MEDICAL DISPENSARY

My mom is a one-woman medical dispensary. She owns all the medicine necessary to treat a boo-boo, manage arthritis, or heal a headache. And she's not afraid to use it.

Back in the 70s when I was a kid, you weren't allowed to get hurt unless Mom could cover it with a Band-Aid or ice pack. In those days, the medicine chest contained calamine lotion, iodine, and Mercurochrome. You could either be pink or red. Both would cover the blood.

Getting the chickenpox was a rite of passage. Before the vaccine, chickenpox wiped out whole classrooms. I remember the year the district canceled school due to a massive outbreak. At that time, Mom actually begged other moms to bring over their infected kids so you could "get it over with." Then she'd dab a cotton ball overloaded with calamine lotion on all the itchy red spots, painful blisters, and crusts. In five days, it was back to school, lesion free.

In grade school, I skidded my bike down the street

for what felt like half a block. Bloody and bruised, with gravel and dirt ground into my legs, I hobbled home. My mother took one look at me and poured on the Mercurochrome. My legs, distinctive carmine red, sizzled under the antiseptic until bath time. That toxic brew's not even on the market today, "generally not recognized as safe and effective." But back in the 1970s, it did the job.

Whaddya mean not safe? Dabbing owies with something known as "monkey blood" might be dangerous?

Get a cough and congestion? Mom tackled that with a healthy dose of whiskey, honey, sugar, and hot lemon water. If you got a fever to go with the other symptoms, she'd stuff you into an ice bath, hypothermia be damned.

Nowadays, my mother's collection of drugs rivals an apothecary. We visited my Midwest family last summer, and she did not fail to amaze us with her medical reservoir.

I swear, before I even knocked, she pulled the door open then yanked me inside. "Ugh, you look sick," she said as she touched my forehead with her lips and pulled me into an embrace. "I've got some meds for that."

My husband followed as she dragged me by the forearm into the kitchen. *Save me from the madman*, I pleaded with my eyes.

"How long have you been feeling bad?" she said wringing her hands.

A regular Dr. Quinn, medicine woman.

"Actually, I'm fine," I said raising my voice. "Maybe a little sniffle from the plane but otherwise…"

"Nonsense," she said, pulling me so close I could smell her breath mint. I swear to God it was wintergreen. "You look terrible. Let me help."

I stared in wonder as my mom rummaged around in one of those mom drawers with fifty bottles of expired medication. You know the one? It's for moms only, the silver drawer handle nearly torn asunder and contents haphazardly stuffed inside. Who cares about expiration date? Best-used-by date?

"Really Mom," I said stepping back a little. "I'm fine."

Pop.

She stuffed a white pill into my open mouth. I dry-swallowed it right down.

Gulp.

She pecked me on the cheek, then pulled back and stared me in the eyes. "Oh no," she said, eyebrows scrunched up.

"What did you give me?"

High blood pressure meds? Arthritis drugs? Zantac? Speak up, lady!

"Well, we'll know in about four hours," she said in a relaxed manner, shoulders back and chin high. "You'll either have constipation or explosive diarrhea. I've got some meds for that."

And she sauntered off.

So, I waited for the worst, but no dire effects were noted, and I got twelve hours of the best sleep in my entire life.

Thank you, Zyrtec allergy meds.

CLUELESS IN PARIS

"Débarquer du train," bellowed across the speaker on the Paris Metro.

"What's happening?" my mother said, wringing her hands.

"No idea," I said, shaking my head. "Just stay put."

"Débarquer du train," was broadcast a second time. Standing passengers swung forward in unison as the brakes screeched to a halt. A sea of black trench coats grabbed their belongings and raced for the nearest exit. My mother and I held hands as we watched people exit the train like salmon going upstream, pushing and squeezing past others.

We had been in Paris only one day. We decided to venture out like a true Parisian, using public transportation, le métro.

We were not prepared.

I scanned the Metro map clutched in my mother's hand.

"What should we do?" she said, picking at her fingernails.

"I have no idea," I said, looking around as the passengers rushed out. "Let's wait a minute."

Before we could say "oh snap," we were the last passengers still on board. A lithe, dark-haired lady standing on the platform took pity on us and stepped back aboard.

"You need to switch trains," she said, with just the hint of a French accent. "Mechanical breakdown. Happens all the time. Follow me."

We plucked our oversized purses off the seat and trailed behind her. She pointed to our map.

"Where are you going?" she said in a soft voice.

"We were on our way to the Musée du Louvre," I said.

"Take the green line and then switch to the yellow," she said. "I'm headed in the same direction. Follow me."

We raced behind as her heels click-clacked down a hallway and up a staircase. "Wait there for the next train," she pointed. "Au revoir." In a puff, she melted away in a flurry of trendy leather boots and fashionable handbags.

We made it to our destination without further incident.

How did we end up clueless in Paris you ask?

Six months prior, on my December birthday, my husband handed me a scroll wrapped with a red ribbon. Inside it said, "Happy Birthday. Enjoy Paris with your mother." A chance to escape the hassles of motherhood and reconnect with my mother in a far-off city of lights filled with art and food appealed to all my senses.

Say no more. I'm out of here!

As fast as a kid scrambling for candy, I organized a nine-day trip to Paris, before my hubby realized he had lost his mind. I used all his frequent flyer points and scored us a hotel and plane tickets.

Can't stop me now!

He had no idea what it meant to care day and night for our seven-year-old son and ten-year-old daughter. What with juggling their school schedule and after-school routine, he'd never offer something like this again.

I must work fast.

"Guess what?" I said to my mother by phone. "We're going to Paris. Mike's sending us with his blessings," I said. "Do you know any French?"

"Not a single word."

On the days leading up to our departure, we practiced saying oh la la, merci beaucoup, oui, and au revoir.

"Bonjour Madame," I said to my mother on my daily phone call. "C'mon talley voo seh mahtan?"

"Wha?" she said, fumbling for an answer. I could just visualize her eyebrows squished as she frowned into the phone.

"How are you this morning?" I said. "Remember? We're supposed to be practicing our French. You need to do your part."

"I'm watching *The French Chef* on television. Not helping much but I know how to make a fabulous French Onion Soup. Adios."

Oh brother. A little dash of Spanish.

Becoming fluent in French in six months or less was as impossible as wiggling your ears, but still we ventured on.

Can we survive with just hello, goodbye, and thank you?

I flew from California to St. Louis Lambert Airport to meet up with my mom, so we could travel together to Paris. From Charles De Gaulle Airport, we taxied to the Paris Hilton Hotel. A snazzy doorman decked out in a long black blazer with shiny brass buttons and a black top hat sporting a white band met the cab and carried our luggage into the lobby.

After we checked in, a bellman announced, "Mademoiselle, please follow me to your room."

Once inside our room, we "oohed" and "aahed" at the sight out the window. If we strained just a tiny bit, we got a clear shot of the Eiffel Tower. Sleek and modern, our room contained two beds with snappy white comforters with a brown band.

Mom eyed the area under the dresser. "Can I use the minibar?" she said tripping over her luggage in her excitement to open the tiny refrigerator door.

"Of course," I said. "But the prices are exorbitant. Let's just take a soda or two and refill it later." We enjoyed a Coke and chilled out on the veranda.

This is the life.

Each morning, Aldo, the concierge, gleefully answered all questions.

"Where's the best shopping?"

"Can you get us show tickets?"

"How do we walk to the Metro?"

There was nothing he couldn't resolve.

By the end of the nine days, we were expert sightseers, navigating public transportation to the Eiffel Tower, Notre-Dame, Musee d'Orsay, Versailles Palace, and Giverny.

On our departure date, we hauled our bags to the lobby, ready for check out.

"Madam, did you enjoy your stay at the Paris Hilton?" said Aldo.

"We had a fabulous time," said my mother. "Thank you so much for your help," she said, handing him a generous tip.

After saying our goodbyes, the checkout process began. Colette, as it prominently announced on her nametag, assisted. She handed me our final bill printed on several sheets of Paris Hilton stationary. I took a cursory look.

What's this?

"Pardon me. What's the 350 euros for?" I asked as my palms broke out in a sweat.

"Minibar expenses."

"May I see an itemized list?"

With a flick of a few keys, a sheet of paper whirred out of the printer. She pushed it across the desk.

What's this? Cigarettes, condoms, cigars, vodka, mixed nuts, ten cans of soda?

"Um, there must be some mistake," I said, with my mother by my side. "We didn't use any of this."

My mother avoided eye contact and moved a few feet away as I continued to argue with the front desk clerk.

"Colette, I'm here alone with my mother," I said as I felt a flush rush across my chest. "Condoms? Cigars? No way."

I felt my mother cringe by my side. "Mom, did you use any of this?"

Her face turned blank as she looked down at her hands.

"Mom?"

Speak up, woman.

"I may have pulled that stuff out just to check it out," she said, blinking rapidly.

"Madam, each time you pulled out an item, your room was charged," Colette piped up from behind the desk. "I'll see what I can do to remove the charges."

With a snap of her head, she rolled her eyes as if to say, "Foolish Americans."

As Colette revised our bill, I asked my mother, "When did this happen?"

"You were taking a shower, and I was curious. I had no idea we would be billed. Soooooooorry."

We waved goodbye and zoomed off to the airport. We'll always have Paris, but Rick Steves never mentioned a single warning about the dangers of the minibar.

NEAR CHRISTMAS BIRTHDAY BLUES

The world is divided into two types of people: those with a birthday on or near Christmas and everyone else.

By the time you celebrate a birthday on or near Christmas, everyone's broke, out of town or forgets about your birthday altogether.

As a young child, I remember being stuck unwrapping my birthday gifts on Christmas day. It didn't matter if we celebrated Christmas at our house or at a relative's place. A sour look would cross their faces when they remembered I had a birthday in two days and they had no intention of being there.

"Here you go," said my cousin, Debbie, handing me a present poorly wrapped in Santas. "We won't have time to come back over in two days. Happy birthday."

Some even dared to rip off a gift tag right in front of me.

"Merry Christmas," Grandma said, slapping a new birthday gift tag over the Christmas one. "Happy birthday," she says with a wink. "This gift is for both."

The classic two-in-one gift.

Not only did I get gypped with one gift, but the darn thing had to be wrapped in Christmas paper too? Visitors made you feel guilty for being born so close to Christmas.

"Gosh, honey," my aunt tut-tutted with sympathy. "We're broke from all the Christmas shopping. Can we make up for it later?"

Oh sure. Like next Christmas?

I'll never forget my Tenth Birthday Bummer. Not a single balloon announced my impending birthday. No lingering smells of birthday cake. Not even one measly present in sight.

"When are we going to celebrate my birthday?" I said in a flat monotone voice and held my breath.

Speechless, Mom covered her face with her hands, snapped up her purse, and made for the door. An hour later, she waltzed into the house, bearing a carrot cake and candles. That's right. December birthday cakes are in short supply at the grocery store.

Good grief woman, you only have one kid!

Forget about having a birthday party on your actual date or anywhere near the date. Your friends are out of school, on vacation, or just plain busy.

When I became an adult, my birthday continued to get buried under Christmas trappings and holiday glee. On my forty-fifth birthday, things spiraled out of control.

That year, since our kids still believed in Santa, we trekked to the Midwest to share their wonder with the grandparents. Towing gifts galore, we visited our two sets of divorced parents.

Do the math. That's four households!

That year we schlepped across the country after Christmas on December 27, my birthday.

Waking up youngsters at 4:00 AM is not an easy task. The 7:00 AM flight from Denver to Peoria, Illinois did not go as planned. Our flight, diverted to Chicago for "equipment problems," caused our initial difficulties. Then due to severe weather, the airline shut down, and the only way to travel was by rental car.

Between Chicago and Peoria, our rental car popped a tire, sending us careening off the highway. If you think it's impossible to get AAA in the middle of a snowstorm, you'd be right.

After nineteen hours of travel, we arrived at Nana's, bearing six suitcases, boxes of gifts, soggy, and exhausted.

Once we said our initial hellos and gathered our breath, I spied a birthday cake on the kitchen table.

"Look," I said as I nudged my husband in the ribs. "Your mom remembered. I want to get at that cake."

At that moment, his mom entered the kitchen and said, "You guys hungry? We tried to wait. Want leftovers?"

My family of four chowed down on a mish mash of leftovers: hunks of turkey hanging off the bone, bits of corn casserole, and a few tablespoons of mashed potatoes. No one whispered a word about the cake.

"Wait," said my daughter with a frown. "It's mom's birthday. We still need to sing."

This kid is definitely my favorite.

"Let's celebrate Mom's birthday tomorrow when Aunt Jean can come back over with the kids. They waited forever for you guys to get here."

I want my mommy!

Day two was more of the same.

After breakfast on day three, I spied the cake looking flatter and less perky than the day before. I tapped my husband on the shoulder and said, "Follow me."

In the kitchen I whispered, "Look," I said, clenching my teeth. "It's been three days since my actual birthday. If you don't start singing and serve this cake, I'm going to push it on the floor."

His eyes bulged as I slowly the edged the cake across the table. As I paused with one finger on the cake, he belted out, "Happy birthday to you, happy birthday to you, happy birthday to Stacey, happy birthday to you."

Before he was finished singing, everyone ran into the room to see what the commotion was about.

My man knows to take me at my word.

To this day, my husband claims I'm a big baby and he believes that everyone actually overcompensates by giving me more gifts.

That's what he said.

BLUE APRON STRESS

This is what I believe: my mother has a great sense of humor, knows what she likes, and returns every single present she's ever received. The reasons for her displeasure ran the gamut from too expensive and too extravagant to too technical and too confusing.

Just too something.

Last Christmas, I gave her a Keurig single serve coffee maker. With a frown and a heavy sigh, she said, "Save your money. I already have a coffee pot."

Don't worry, my feelings are not hurt.

Even a cashmere sweater raised her ire.

"Mom that color really brings out the green in your eyes."

She said, "You keep it. Too fancy."

But for the first time, I discovered a birthday gift she would be hard-pressed to criticize.

Blue Apron, a popular meal kit delivery service, arrived in time for her special day. For four months, my husband and I had used this delivery service with fantastic results. It provided fresh, pre-portioned ingredients to your doorstep with the spices necessary to prepare homemade quality meals in twenty-five minutes or less. What's not to love?

Anxious to share my newfound meal kit delivery service with my mother, I shared the news. "Mom, I'm cooking decent meals again," I said during our regular phone call. "Mike loves Blue Apron."

"Tell me more," she said, shushing her boyfriend in the background.

On and on I relayed my foray into exotic dinners. Roasted pork and summer succotash, scrumptious. Pan-friend Françoise-style chicken, easy peasy. Hoisin beef and vegetable stir-fry, time to call Chef Ramsey.

She said, "Sounds so yummy. Email me the information." I sent her the Blue Apron website and even attached pictures of our lavish meals.

Next, I sent her a trial box. I reasoned that together with her boyfriend, they could prepare healthy meals in record time. No more last-minute jaunts to the grocery store.

Boy was I wrong.

"How's it going, Mom? Did you get my package?" I said by phone, waiting for her to express her gratitude.

"A big box is sitting right here on the counter," she said, tension in her voice. "Says Blue Apron on the outside."

You're welcome.

"That's it. Open it."

"Why's it so heavy? What's in here?"

Geez, she's acting like she got a package from al-Qaeda.

"Oh, brother! It's filled with ice packs, chicken, veggies, everything you need to cook two meals," I said, thinly masking my irritation. "Just open it."

What's with the attitude? She should be thanking me!

"What do you think?" I said after a moment of silence passed.

"Look. I can't talk right now," she snapped. "Gotta figure out how to put all this crap into the refrigerator. Blue Apron stressed me out." She clicked off without so much as a good-bye.

What's the big deal, I thought? Throw the stuff in the refrigerator until you're ready to make it. It's as simple as it gets.

In several days, I called for a follow-up.

"How were the meals?" I said through pursed lips.

"Oh, I never made them," she said. "I put the meat in the freezer. Had to throw out most of the vegetables. Maybe when you come to town, we'll make it together."

What the hell's she talking about? I live 3,000 miles away.

"Gosh, Mom. I wanted to do something nice for you."

"Well, I'm glad it worked out for YOU, but all that food. The bags, the boxes. So many ice packs. What am I supposed to do with all that stuff?"

"Just follow the recycling instructions. No big deal."

Seriously, woman, is this the hardest thing you've ever had to deal with?

"I appreciate the thought but please don't send it again," she said with a sigh. "Keep your money. Blue Apron stressed me out. I thought you said this was easy."

In the future, I'm sending her gift certificates. Impersonal and returnable, just the way she likes it.

THE HUNDRED-FOOT JOURNEY

Like the Griswolds in *National Lampoon's Vacation*, our family was on a quest, and along the way things got complicated. Who knew going one hundred feet could take five hours?

My husband and I yearned to share the magic of Ireland with our daughter and son on our annual summer vacation. Our group did traditional sightseeing, toured the Guinness Factory in Dublin, listened to Irish music at the local pubs, and explored the Rock of Cashel.

Nothing could prepare us for the beauty of our final destination, the Gap of Dunloe. Located in the town of Killarney, County Kerry, the Gap was nestled amidst panoramic views of rugged mountains, waterfalls, and expansive powder-blue skies. Below these lay the world-famous Lakes of Killarney—Lough Leane, Muckross Lake, and Upper Lake.

We were ready to see its legendary beauty, but our daughter had different plans.

"Can't we do something else?" said Ashley, our pony-tailed teenager, with a heavy sigh. "Five hours is a long time to get to a castle. The other brochure says we can drive there in minutes."

"The lady at the front desk told me that we have to join a tour group to see it," I explained through gritted teeth. Ross Castle, a 15th-century tower house, was situated on the edge of Lough Leane. The Irish pamphlet called it "a must-see."

"Ugh, I'd rather take a nap," she said, flopping down on the nearest chair.

In the morning, we were picked up by bus at our hotel, The Malton.

"Mom, here comes our ride," my son said in a loud voice. "It looks like an old-fashioned ambulance."

In place of a Red Cross sign dangled a banner, "Gap of Dunloe & Lakes of Killarney Adventure." Four windows on each side and elongated front grill, our vehicle held eight passengers, and the driver.

After an hour, our bus driver dropped us off at the base of the Gap of Dunloe in Killarney National Park. Since cars were banned from the Gap, we could either ride bikes, walk, or take a jaunting car, a four occupant two-wheeled carriage pulled by a single horse.

Guess what our brood picked?

At this point, a local man, Shamus, rugged and tanned with a friendly smile, offered us his jaunting car. "Cheers," he said in a deep voice.

"Need a ride up the Gap?" he said, as he sized us up and down. His expression implied, "Holy crap, they grow them big in the States."

"This is Sally," he said, patting the flank of his horse, a sturdy, hard-working draught horse with coarse brown hair and white markings near the hoofs.

"Cover up with the blankets to keep the rain off ye," he said, tossing a tarp our way. A musty, dusty smell assaulted our nostrils as we brushed dirt away.

He schlepped us for six miles along the muddy road, up and down steep hills, singing Irish ditties and sharing local history.

"Over in Killarney, many years ago/ Me Mither sang a song to me in tones so sweet and low," he serenaded, as the jaunting car rocked to and fro, mud squishing out the wheels. His deep Irish accent echoed through the Gap, melodious and charming.

After miles, the jaunting slowed as the road grew steeper and Sally began to struggle. At this point, Shamus, his rosy face and red hair peeking beneath his cap, jumped off and jogged alongside Sally to alleviate weight. By my account, she hauled 750-pounds of Gustafson, plus Shamus.

"Maybe you should get out as well," I said to Mike, poking him in the ribs and pointing out Shamus, running alongside Sally. "He's got to be at least seventy years old."

"Fine," Mike said. "Shamus, would you like me to get out and walk?"

"Poor Sally would surely appreciate that," he said.

Our carriage ride took about two hours to go seven miles to our first destination, Lower Killarney, a lake that leads to the Atlantic

Next, we hiked one mile to get to the second leg of our journey, a ride on a fourteen passenger Jon boat. Stuffed with soggy, weary passengers outfitted in orange life jackets, our vessel slogged along. We passed rocky scenery of slate and granite laced banks.

After two hours, Ross Castle came into view.

"Finally," said Ashley. "Can't wait to get some pictures."

At this point, our driver hollered, "Folks, you better

run when we land. You have five minutes to board the vans back to your hotel."

"Are you kidding me?" Ashley said. "This was the only part I cared about." She blasted out of the Jon boat, and in a flash of blond hair, dashed toward the castle ruins like it was a Blue Light Special at Wal-Mart.

Snap. Click. Ka-chick. She snapped pictures with her iPhone.

"Hurry, hurry," I yelled, flagging my family from the steps of the van. I was the parent assigned to hold the van.

My crew embarked, water spraying the interior of the van off their jackets and umbrellas.

"How long is this going to be?" said my daughter.

"No idea. May be at least another hour to get back to our place."

Our van turned left out of the parking lot and in the distance we glimpsed The Malton. This whole time we were less than one mile away from our hotel. We had navigated in a huge circle for five hours and ended up one mile away.

My daughter was right. Drats!

"Told you, Mom. We wasted the whole day getting to Ross Castle down the street from the hotel," she said, as I shuffled away. "Hey, where you going?"

"Off to take a nap."

DOWNSIZING CHRISTMAS

Fifty-two years ago, my mother festooned a real tree with sixty pounds of ornaments, tinsel, and twinkling lights plus adorned the inside of our house with forty-nine nutcrackers, nineteen Santas, nine hand-knitted stockings, eighteen electric candles, and an endless assortment of gaudy trinkets that sparkled, glowed, or danced.

My father controlled the outside decorations with enough Christmas paraphernalia to shut down the entire block's power grid. He blanketed the front of our place with lights; bubbled, frosted, tiny, and otherwise. He randomly covered it all, from gutters and porch rails to bushes and trees. Like a t-shirt cannon at the ballgame, lights spit all over the front of our home. Who cares? That's how you decorated in the 1970s, fire hazard be damned.

Once I got married and had children of my own, I paid attention as my mom quietly purged the holiday clutter.

Weeks before Christmas we dropped in for a visit.

"Hey, what happened to our old tree?" I asked, plucking a tiny ornament from the bough of a new two-foot artificial one perched on an end table.

"Had to scale back," she said, hands on hips. "Couldn't handle that big one any longer. Plus, after Christmas, I can just throw a Hefty bag over the top and carry it downstairs."

Ah, I loved that tree.

Soon the two-footer disappeared too and was replaced with a sixteen-inch ceramic tree.

The ultimate grandma tree.

During her last visit to California, I inquired about her downsizing Christmas strategy.

"How are you decorating for Christmas these days?" I asked.

"Wreath on the front door," she said with a smile and a nod.

I finally get it.

Downsizing Christmas has its appeal. After doing Christmas for twenty-seven years, I realized that my mother had latched onto a good thing.

Back when my husband and I were newlyweds, our toughest decision at Christmas was live versus artificial tree. Dressed up in our warmest attire, we tromped through the tree farms in search of the perfect one. Then we tricked it out with discounted ornaments from Target and my mom's hand-me-downs.

Each night we refilled the tree's bucket with water. But then we went out of town to visit relatives. What did we know? When we returned, the ornaments had slipped down to the bottom branches and it was as dry as my grandma's hands in the winter.

The next year we downsized to a six-foot artificial tree.

Safety first.

Later, we traded that tree in for a newer model with pre-lit white lights, still in use today.

Three weeks before Christmas, my husband hauled our holiday stuff out of storage, fifteen boxes and counting.

"What are we doing?" I said, dabbing the sweat from my brow. "Nobody seems to care. I understand what Mom was talking about. It's just too much."

Our kids have left the nest, daughter works full-time, and our son's a junior in college. Why are we still putting up Christmas?

Then my daughter called me from work and asked, "Can I come over and see the tree?"

"We've been waiting for your call," I said trying to mask my frustration. "We could use your help."

I believe that in a family, one regular-sized tree must come down before another one goes up; it's the circle of Christmas. My mother stopped putting up her tree when I moved out and erected my own. It was my daughter's turn.

After much cajoling, Ashley and her boyfriend arrived, ready to assist. They helped her dad assemble the four pieces of the eight-foot tree and sprinkled the decorations around the house.

Afterwards, I tried to offer Ashley handfuls of ornaments, assorted elves, Santas, and snowmen to take back to her apartment, but she said she had enough decorations, maybe later.

"You keep it," she said as she hugged us goodbye. "I don't have the room in my tiny apartment. But don't worry. I plan on coming home every year to celebrate. You both are Christmas to me."

It looks like my plans for downsizing Christmas

will be put on hold. But Easter's coming up. How many ceramic bunnies does one mom need anyway?

WORLD'S BEST DAUGHTER

My father and my seventy-year-old art teacher prepared to fight Gladiator style in the middle of the college art gallery.

And I could do nothing to stop it.

Like the Robert De Niro and Ben Stiller epic fight scene in *Little Fockers*, the dads challenged each other to combat, at least verbally. There was a lot of poking and prodding.

Let me fill you in on how this started.

My father, tall, gangly, and seventy-two years young, possessed an outgoing and loud personality that demanded attention from anyone within earshot. He visited last summer to view my latest art exhibit. For six years, I studied fine art at the local community college. For a semester, my class prepared oil and acrylic paintings for the "We Can" art exhibit to benefit the area food bank.

Each student auctioned a thirty-six-by-thirty-six-inch painting of their interpretation of the meaning of canned food to the homeless. I labored over my realistic interpretation for months. My painting depicted canned peaches surrounded by fresh peach slices.

Bill, our fearless leader and visual arts coordinator, envisioned the idea. After twenty-eight years of teaching at the college, his retirement was approaching. This exhibit was his last hurrah.

"Dad, maybe some of my friends from class will be at the show," I said, as I glanced around the gallery. "I bet we bump into my art teacher."

We browsed the art collection, pausing from time to time to snap pictures of the students' works.

"Your can is the best," he said, nodding to himself with confirmation.

"Thanks, Dad."

"Here comes my teacher," I said, pointing in his direction. "I must introduce you."

Bill wore a black leather beret tilted to the side and his signature Hawaiian shirt. His bushy eyebrows went up when he noticed me.

"Bill, this is my dad, Charles," I said with a grin. "He's visiting from St. Louis."

As they shook hands, my dad pulled me closer by the shoulders and announced, "This girl right here is the world's best daughter," he said beaming with satisfaction and gripping me even tighter. "She's been damn well nearly perfect her whole life."

"Nope," my teacher said, rocking back on his heels. "My daughter is the world's best."

What's happening?

Dad grabbed hold of Bill's forearm for emphasis and said, "I'm not kidding. Stacey's great. She's the perfect daughter, never a problem."

"I'm not kidding either," Bill said, thrusting out his chest. "My daughter's perfect."

A sword of words unsheathed.

I visually willed my dad to stop by maintaining solid eye contact. But it was too late. I've seen this before. Once he got started, nothing deflected his stampede to elevate my Best Daughter status.

Sorry, Bill.

"She's been a straight-A student her whole life, never a bit of trouble," he said hooking his thumbs in his belt loops, looking Bill directly in the eye.

"Is that so?" Bill said. "I bet she never received the Excellence in Student Leadership Award."

"That's nothing," disputed my father. "This little gal earned a full scholarship to one of the top colleges." He stepped back a few feet and made a fist.

Are they getting ready to duel?

"Well, my kid joined the Peace Corps after college," he said, waving his hand as if to dismiss my father.

For ten minutes, two seventy-something men bantered back and forth, competing to bestow upon their kid, "World's Best Daughter."

A fight to the death.

"Let's call it a tie," I announced, clenching my jaw.

I distracted my father with an abstract painting on the other side of the gallery and used my hand to firmly guide him away from my teacher.

"I apologize for Dad," I said to Bill over my shoulder. "I'm sure Kelly is the World's Best Daughter."

To you.

OTHERS

"Back when I was a kid, you weren't allowed to get hurt unless Mom could cover it with an ice pack or a Band-Aid. And all she had was calamine lotion, iodine, and Mercurochrome. You could either be pink or red, both of which helped hide the blood."

—Stacey Gustafson, *Laugh Out Loud*,
Firehouse Bar and Grill, St. Louis, Missouri

FOR A GOOD TIME, CALL

My dalliance with phone sex came about despite obvious warning signs and my better judgment.

I dedicate five hours each day to write and catch up on social media. Every morning, I gathered my writing journal, iPhone, and coffee, and shuffle upstairs to my lair. Supplies by my side, I plop down to finish my mystery novel.

Click, click.

"What this?! How come nothing's happening?" I said aloud.

Usually, when I'm unable to get Internet access, I call in "The Expert," who happens to be my sixteen-year-old son. Since he was in school, I contacted my next best resource.

"You free?" I asked my friend, Mary, while banging my head on the desk. "I'm on a tight deadline, and my computer won't cooperate."

"I'll be right over," she said with a snort.

Before she even pressed the doorbell, I dragged Mary inside.

"What's going on?" she said, yanking her arm from my grip.

"No idea. When I turn on the computer, it asks for a sixteen-digit password."

Who the heck remembers passwords?! I screamed in my head.

"Maybe your connection's loose," she said and proceeded to unplug and replug each cord from the computer and printer. A few clicks later, the same message appeared on the screen: "Enter your password."

What the hell?

"It could be your router or modem," said Mary looking around my desk.

Speak English, woman. What's a router?

"Let's find out if that's what it is. Do you have a contract with your Internet provider?"

"I've called before, but they ask so many questions I usually end up frustrated," I whined. "But I'll give it a shot again."

I leafed through a pile of notes in my desk drawer and found the phone number for the technical support of our Internet provider, Berserk.com. For $199 per year, your questions were guaranteed to be answered 24/7.

I strapped on my headset and dialed 888-IT-SUCKS. I waited on hold for an hour and was startled when I heard the connection finally pick up. "This is Jason at Technical Support," said a guy with a low voice and slight accent. "How are you?" Within seconds, his picture popped onto my screen.

Live technical support? Weird.

"Fine. You?" I answered.

What's with the chitchat? Chop Chop.

"I'm good. Thanks for asking. How may I assist you today?"

"I think I have a problem with my router."

"What's going on?"

In my sloppy, low-tech way, I translated my crisis to the technician, my best friend Mary by my side for moral support. I told the tech what we had done and that my friend thought the problem must be something bigger.

"My girlfriend thinks I have a corrupt cable connection," I blurted out.

"Tell me more," he said in a slow, suggestive way.

Why's he acting so strange?

"She didn't notice any problems with the hook up and tried again. Nothing happened."

"No," Jason said. "Tell me more about your *girlfriend*."

"What?"

"So, you have a *girlfriend*?"

Is this guy saying what I think he's saying? I just want tech support!

I motioned to Mary to listen in on the call. She pressed her ear against the headset, and her eyes bulged.

"Yes, she's my girlfriend from the neighborhood," I said matter-of-factly.

Mary made a cuckoo motion at her temple. She whispered to me, "Let him talk. Let's see what happens."

Tech support, my ass.

"How long has she been your *girlfriend*?"

"We met about five years ago."

"Is she your *lover*?" he said, smearing the last word so it sounded like "loverrrrrrrrrrr."

Where are you going with this, JASON? My mouth hung agape.

"What are you wearing?" he said. I could almost see his leer.

I mouthed to Mary, "Pervert!"

"Will you Snap Chat me a nude picture?" he asked next.

"Hey, what's your name again?" I asked him, clenching my teeth.

"Jason."

"Where are you?"

"Delhi."

"Well, Jason, I don't think you should be talking to me this way," I said, a little too loudly. "I just need some technical support. I don't wish to deal with your sexual innuendos or have phone sex with you. Is anyone else there I can talk to?"

The longest pause in history ricocheted through the phone lines and across the continents. *Tick tock, buddy.*

"So sorry," he said with a stutter. "Please don't get me in trouble. Let me get back to your problem and try to fix your connection. OK?"

He gained remote access to my computer and had it up and running in no time.

"I'm going to add six months to your contract," he said with a stammer. "Are we good now?"

"Make it a year, and I'll forget the whole thing happened," I said. He agreed. And his icon disappeared in a puff.

Now that's what I call problem-solving!

GALLBLADDER MATTERS

I could never have anticipated that my love for the zesty and cheesy could put me into solitary confinement.

Curious?

I scored my first paid writing assignments as a cookbook critic; I reviewed *California Pizza Kitchen Family Cookbook* with the gusto of Chef Emeril Lagasse. Slinging pizza dough high in the air and stirring sauces, ranging from hot-and-spicy to mild-and-sweet, tantalized the senses.

Hot Jamaican jerk chicken pizza, Chipotle chicken with smoked jalapenos, and Sicilian pizza featuring three different meats and cheeses pleased my family of four. No challenge was too great.

By week two, the cheesy delights resulted in bloating, cramping, spasms, and burning pain in my belly. Like a blackened chili pepper, I was rushed away from the oven and into the emergency room. Final diagnosis, gallbladder attack.

It had to go before it would blow.

At the hospital, a nurse with a tight bun and overplucked eyebrows asked, "Please choose the face that best describes your pain level."

The pain scale showed a series of faces ranging from a happy face, "no hurt" level zero to crying face, "hurts worst" level ten.

"Level eight," I gasped. "Hurts Whole Lot."

"The doctor will see you in a few minutes," she said with a swish of her polyester pantsuit. "Wait here."

Where would I go? I can't even walk.

In strutted Dr. Paine, holding a clipboard and sporting an ink pen firmly planted behind his ear. "How's your cholesterol level?" he asked as he scribbled notes on the pad. "Eat spicy food? Cheese?"

Yeah, Dr. Smarty-pants. I. Love. It. All!!

"Well...um. I eat a little cheese."

In a flash, my fate was sealed. Fat chance I would survive long enough to review another cookbook. No more dairy products, eggs, chocolate, alcohol, onions, red meat, soda, plus about a thousand other no-nos for me.

I left with a list of all the food groups eliminated from my diet and a date scheduled for surgery.

Two weeks later, the gallbladder removal left an incision mark as tiny as the end of a pencil eraser. After a few hours in recovery, my husband drove me home. He served me soup, and I napped for three hours. By nighttime, I popped into the family room as my gang binged on *Modern Family*.

"Hey, Mom," said my daughter, one hand in a popcorn bowl and the other glued to her iPhone. "You feeling better?"

"Not too bad," I said, patting my belly.

By day two, I hopped up out of bed, made breakfast for my crew and caught fifteen minutes of *The View*.

Mama's back.

I thought *This is a piece of cake*. I don't need any more meds. What's all the fuss about? My friends and family forked over bad advice.

Then my stomach cramped, sharp and achy. My abdomen twitched as I held onto the wall to get off the sofa.

Oh crap. What have I done?

I stumbled into the kitchen, clawing at my Vicoden prescription and gulped down two pills with a full glass of water.

That should do it.

I tried to be brave when my husband came into the room.

"You don't look too good," he said. "What's going on?"

Oh, you think so genius! I. Am. Dying.

"Agonizing pain," I said letting out a whimper. "Let's pray this damn pill works."

Ay caramba! I dropped to the ground.

"MUST GET TO THE HOSPITAL NOW," I yelled rolling into a ball.

My husband guided me to the car, and I cursed the full twenty minutes to the hospital.

He tried his best to focus on the road and look anywhere but at my body writhing in the passenger seat.

He dumped me off at Emergency. Nurse Hornrims pushed me into a wheelchair and processed me at the front desk. Where was my husband?

Could he be any slower?

"What's your name? What your birthday?"

What if I punch you in the throat? I was here two days ago.

She continued to rattle off a million questions as I moaned and writhed in the wheelchair.

Someone's going to pay.

"Can't my husband answer these questions? He's parking the car."

"Sorry but it must come from the patient. Only one more question."

Hornrims asked, "Which face best represent your level?"

"What's higher than a ten? I feel like someone's trying to dig out my entrails with nail clippers," I screamed.

After the interrogation ended, they pushed me to the emergency room, my husband following.

I hollered as I passed the other patients peeking from behind the curtains in the emergency room.

Where the hell are they taking me?

Finally, she halted and used a key to open a metal door. She whispered something to my husband like "She'll be happier here" and then left. With a clang, the door shut behind her.

Solitary confinement.

In between moans, I squinted up at my husband, "They gave me my own room?"

"Think they were worried that you were disturbing the other patients," he said in a matter-of-fact way.

"Get the drugs," I continued to moan.

The nurse strolled in, pushing an IV stand with a bag of meds hanging from a pole.

I love you.

She inserted a needle into a vein in my wrist that delivered immediate, fast-acting relief.

Thank you, Jesus.

My cries wound down to a whimper.

"She can go now," the nurse said to my husband as she checked her watch and held the door open.

"That's it?" he said blowing out his cheeks.

"Yes. Please go. Now."

Get me out of here.

As he pushed me down the corridor past the other patients, I heard faint applause. And it wasn't because they were happy I was feeling better.

SHAKE, RATTLE, AND ROLL

Self-identified Midwesterners generally consider Indiana, Iowa, Illinois, Michigan, Wisconsin, Minnesota, Ohio, Missouri, and Kansas to be one of their own. These residents are tough-minded, pugnacious, and rugged. I'm proud to call the Midwest my birthplace.

Natural disasters like tornados, flash floods, hail, and ice storms regularly hit the Midwest. Heck, it's home to storm chasers, guys who follow tornados just for fun. Unpaid.

With our ability to find a silver lining and look for the positive, that ain't no biggie.

A tough group of SOB's.

When I moved from the Midwest to California about fifteen years ago, I was prepared for severe Midwest weather, but earthquakes, not so much. Sure, in Missouri we get a rumble now and then, but it's quickly overshadowed by the ice storm of the century or news that a 400-pound feral hog attacked a family.

No weather's going to bring down the Heartland.

In contrast, I consider Californians a bunch of softies. *There. I said it.*

At dinner with six other couples, at least three native

to California, I asked, "What's the worst weather you've ever experienced?"

"Well," my friend said flipping her blond tresses over her shoulder, "once in San Francisco, the temperature got down to forty."

Are you kidding woman? That's the best you got?

For me, below thirty degrees is snow skiing weather. In college, my boyfriend, and now husband, and I bought lift tickets for Baraboo, Wisconsin with our last bit of cash. Devil's Head Resort sported minus thirty-degree weather in December. Their snowmaker actually stopped working because it was too cold to run. That weekend we wore a facemask, thermal undies, and heat pads inside our gloves and braved the conditions.

Now that's what I'm talking about.

In California, our suburban neighborhood is composed of Silicon Valley tech employees—smart people but not familiar with severe weather. After all, it's the home of 24/7 sunshine. In California when it rains, windshield wipers don't even click on.

Our friends were a mixed bag of local natives and many from as far as India. I found that most had never experienced extreme weather.

Crazy Eddie, a nearby neighbor, wearing flip-flops, khaki cargo shorts, and a worn grey t-shirt that read "Jesus Is My Homeboy," limped across the street as I pulled my trashcans to the curb.

"How you doing Ed," I said. "Looks like you're hurt."

"It's nothing," he said with a *whatever* shrug. "Sprained my ankle paddle-boarding. Got a question for you."

"Sure," I said as he edged closer. "Shoot."

"What's your earthquake plan?"

What? I need to plan?

Then he held me captive for the next five minutes with his road map to surviving the Big One.

"I've buried a fifty-gallon drum of water in the backyard," he said, thumbs wrapped around his belt loops. "And all eight kids have an emergency backpack with a five-day supply of rations. What's your plan?"

Shake, rattle, and roll.

"Me," I said, waving a hand in dismissal. "I don't have a plan. I just need to keep YOUR address in MY pocket."

His eyes grew wide, and he turned on his heel dragging his can back home.

Better have enough rations for four more, mister!

I ATTRACT WEIRDOS

As you may have figured out by now, I am a regular stay-at-home soccer mom; average weight, mousy blond hair, and a lover of comfortable clothing, like yoga pants, t-shirts, and jackets. I drive the ultimate mom vehicle, a blue Honda minivan, and my husband thinks I'm too friendly and approachable.

Like that's a thing?

I'll come right out and say it. I attract weirdos.

After we moved to Colorado, we hosted an open house to meet the new neighbors. I invited everyone within a two-block radius, including Ann from across the street.

You see, once we moved in, other neighbors warned me about Ann.

"She's loony tunes," said Beth, another mom from up the street. "I heard she was spotted swimming in a neighbor's pool when they went out of town. Naked. Just plain weird."

Ann burst into our party carrying an oversized purse.

"Isn't she acting odd?" I asked my husband, wiggling my pinky in her direction.

"You invited her," he said, cupping one hand over

his mouth. "Keep an eye out."

I gawked from across the room as Ann systematically cruised down our buffet table, filled two gallon-sized Ziploc bags with mushroom appetizers, mozzarella sticks, buffalo chicken wings, and fiesta pinwheels. She even bundled away a chunk of baked Brie plus Ritz crackers.

What the hell was that?

She stuffed my treats into her purse, breezed by me in a puff of garlic and hot sauce, and high tailed it out the door.

You could say I had that one coming since I invited her over. But it doesn't matter if I know them or not, freaks find me.

Take a trip to Taco Bell for my growing son's fifth meal of the day.

Outside the fast-food joint, we spotted a perfect opportunity to put charity into motion. A twenty-something homeless-looking man sat on the ground near the front door, holding a white poster board.

"Brock, here's an opportunity to help others," I said, as I handed my son some money. "Just do like we talked about earlier."

He ambled over, throwing me a knowing glance over his shoulder.

"Sir," he said maintaining strong eye contact. "Would you like me to buy you something to eat?"

"No," the guy said as he looked at the ground. "I'm fine."

"Um, okay. Here, you can have this," he said and dropped five dollars into the homeless guy's jar.

I reached the front door and squinted at his sign.

Wait a minute!

"Can I take a closer look at your sign?" I asked. He held it in my direction.

"Are you kidding me?" I said raising my face. "NEED MONEY FOR SCOTTISH FESTIVAL!"

"Just trying to keep it real, lady," he said.

But my most unusual interaction with an oddball had to be in the parking lot at Target.

I parked my car near the entrance. My friend, Lori, pulled her minivan next to mine, honked and waved.

"Hey, fancy seeing you here," I said, clutching my purse as I headed toward the entrance.

"Want to grab a coffee after shopping?"

"Sure," she said. Then she gawked over my head. "There's a lady's marching straight at you. Know her?"

"Nope," I said, pulling my purse closer to my chest. "Maybe she's coming over to you."

"No way. You attract freaks. She's staring right at you."

My friend edged to the side of her car as the lady lurched closer.

"Can you do me a favor?" the dark-haired woman asked with a penetrating stare.

"Sure," I said.

"Could you stay by my car and watch my baby as I run inside a few minutes?"

"Um…huh? Wait, I don't think this is a good idea. I better not."

My friend withdrew even further into the shadows.

The woman stormed away, yanked open the back door of her car, and pulled out her baby. She glanced backward with a mean face and hauled ass into the store.

"See, told ya. You attract freaks."

She's right.

I'm a freak magnet. My guess is I'll keep meeting the strange and unusual assortment of oddballs at parking lots, fast food joints, and neighborhood events. Plus, I'll never run out of material for my stories, and always have a tale to tell at a party. But for now, I'm packing pepper spray as a precaution.

I SPY WITH MY LITTLE EYE

We scanned the marquee at the local movie theater. Action, comedy, drama, romance, the choices were endless. My husband's idea of a perfect flick featured massive bloodshed, violence, explosions, guns, knives, fast cars, and trashy girls. My nerves couldn't take another *Natural Born Killers* episode. My hands shook for days and nightmares disrupted my sleep for weeks after that one.

"What are you in mood for?" said Mike.

We compromised on Melissa McCarthy's *Spy*.

"I'll grab some popcorn and meet you inside. Aisle seat," said Mike, heading toward concessions.

I surveyed the cinema before I scooted midway up to snag primo aisle seats. In my book, nothing's worse than being trapped in the middle seats. What's the proper protocol if you need to make mad dash to the bathroom after chugging a thirty-two-ounce soda? Do I hit moviegoers in the face with my massive rear or scamper out, crotch to the face?

I digress.

Once seated, I squinted toward the entrance waiting for Mike. A few rows down, I eyeballed our good friend,

Jim, making his way alone up the steps.

"Hmmm, wonder where Joanne is?" I thought.

Joanne and Jim were a cute couple, very compatible and clearly in love. Each spring and summer, baseball connected our families. Since our sons were second graders, we celebrated our kids wins and losses on the bleachers, sharing healthy snacks and high fives.

I squinted again. Trailing behind Jim was a blond bombshell. With a huge smile, she "excuse me" and "pardon me" down the aisle to the seats in the row behind us.

Hey, what's going on here?

Popcorn in hand, my husband reached our seats five minutes later, plopped the armrest down, and promptly slurped his mega drink.

"Hey, Jim from baseball's sitting in the row behind us but I think he's with another woman," I whispered in his ear, blocking my face behind the jumbo popcorn bucket.

"Can't tell," said Mike, offhandedly glancing behind.

By now the previews began, and cell phones were silenced as the theater fell into a half-darkened state. My husband snuggled deep into his plush seat, tilted his head back, and let out a sigh.

To get a better look behind me, I stood up and I draped my coat carefully over the back of the headrest then peeked out the corner of my eye.

Call me Bond, James Bond.

"Yep, that's definitely Jim," I said touching my fingertips together in a steeple. "And it's not his wife."

What to do? What to do?

"Take a look for yourself," I said, poking him in the ribs.

"Forget about it. Leave it alone. Probably his sister

or something."

Of course, he would say that. He's a man.

"Damn, I can't tell for sure if it's Joanne. Should I call her?" I said, iPhone clamped in my sweaty palm, finger poised above my contacts.

If I call her now, she will have time to catch him red-handed.

"Leave it alone," he said, stuffing a gigantic handful of popcorn in his mouth.

"Be right back. Going to the restroom," I said, half standing.

"Sit. Back. Down."

"Fine, but if this turns out to be an affair, it will be all your fault. Hope you can live with yourself."

"I'm okay with that."

After the movies, we stayed to watch the trailer. I peeked behind me.

Drats! Too slow. They're gone.

We plodded down the staircase to the main lobby.

"Can you believe it?" I said to my husband.

"What?"

"About Jim and Joanne?"

"You still worrying about that? Let's get out of here," Mike said, trashing his stray popcorn bucket and empty cup.

Across the lobby, Jim appeared. I gawked as he pushed straight toward me like RoboCop hunting Arnold Schwarzenegger.

"Hey, guys. How's it going?" he said with big smile on his face.

"Oh…um…hello…Jim. Nice to see you."

He's pretty brazen to bring his "girlfriend" over to meet us.

"How's it going, Stacey?" said the other woman.

How does she know my name?

I soaked in a long look at the hussy. She had some nerve prancing around with a married man. All of a sudden, she came into focus.

"Joanne, is that you? I hardly recognized you," I said, with a stutter.

"I get that all the time," she said patting her hair. "I changed things up and decided to go blond. Like it?"

"Um, yeah."

"What did you think of the movie?"

"Closer to real life than you can imagine."

Case closed.

SOMEWHAT IRRATIONAL FEARS

Some people have irrational fears, like fear of heights, spiders, or public speaking. When survival instincts kick in, we go from calm to paranoid in a microsecond. My phobia was scelerophobia, fear of burglars, bad men or crime in general. This causes me to check and recheck hotel locks. Constantly being vigilant is exhausting.

Since I usually travel out of town with my husband, I'm a bit of a novice when it comes to overnight excursions alone, but one thing I understand perfectly is personal safety. My accommodations at the Marriott in Dayton, Ohio for the *Erma Bombeck Writers' Workshop* had all the essential amenities, free shampoo, complementary breakfast, and no husband or kids. Hotel locks upon initial inspection appeared in working order.

Around midnight, before I snuggled into the plush duvet and prepared to hog the entire bed, I pulled down the shades and locked the door and windows. Then I double-checked the door locks one last time. Chain in place, check. Deadbolt activated, check.

Wait a minute.

When I rotated the deadbolt to the right, nothing happened. No little click. Nada. I turned and checked, turned and checked. The distinctive click never occurred. I even opened the door and stared at the outline of a deadbolt nub on the doorjamb.

Why won't this stupid thing pop out?

I tiptoed around the bed, clutched the phone, and called the operator. On the other end of the phone line, I detected a buzz buzz rather than the familiar ring tone, briiing briiing.

Most assuredly, the line was D.E.A.D.

I'm no dummy. I read enough murder mysteries to know the ending to this scene.

Someone's waiting in the hallway to murder me. Not falling for this one.

My heart rate elevated, and my hands trembled.

Since it was 10:00 PM, well past the time management could fix my problem, I barricaded the door with an end table, ice bucket, and the Holy Bible.

Take that, bad guy.

In the morning after a restless night filled with elaborate nightmares of being chased by zombies and bitten by daddy longlegs, I contacted the front desk with my iPhone. "Excuse me," I said glancing at the digital clock on the night table. "The deadbolt is broken, and the phone doesn't work. Do you think maintenance could repair it by the time I return from the workshop?"

"No problem," he said with a heavy sigh.

Don't let me disturb you.

For two more nights, the phone remained dead and the bolt remained AWOL. My anxiety continued to rise. Could the bad guys break in and steal my autographed books? What if they smothered me in my sleep? Or worse, what if I get locked inside the tiny hotel room and can't get to the free buffet?

By the third day, my complaints earned me a gift basket filled with a bottle of wine, chips, and snack bars. Plus, a friendly note.

Hey, how'd they get in my room?

> *Good morning Ms. Gustafson. I wanted to let you know that we had Adam from our engineering department look at your phone and dead bolt. Both are in working order so you will be safe from the Grandpa Big Foot. Now the deadbolt works a little differently than the standard dead bolt as this one is electronic, so when you turn the lock it will activate the dead bolt that is already out, so you will not hear the 'click' when it locks. For the phone, you will need to press the talk or speaker button, and then dial the number. You won't hear a dial tone or anything until after the number has been dialed and it starts ringing.*
>
> *P.S. I thoroughly look forward to reading, "Are You Kidding Me?" and passing it on to my special someone once I get my hands on a copy.*

Suffice it to say, I'm still uncertain as to what happened. Maybe it was a case of user error or Grandpa Big Foot?

But one thing I know, you can never be too safe. Bring mace.

POTTERY BARN DEBACLE

Redecorating is as stressful as losing your cell phone. It sucks up your day, it's going to cost you more than you want to spend, and your husband's not going to be pleased.

Months ago, I researched Pottery Barn's website for lighting. Their home furnishing choices ranged from patio tables, sofas, and kitchenware to bedding, mirrors, and general décor. Lamp selections were more numerous than paint samples at Home Depot.

I measured and analyzed my newly redecorated den to select the best lamp. Should I go with brass or silver? Floor or table lamp? Traditional or transitional?

After studying the selections as carefully as a professor prepares a calculus final, it was go time. I added to the cart one floor lamp plus a shade.

Since when do lamps come without shades? Whatever.

The website said my order would be mailed immediately. But soon things started to unravel.

Two weeks later, I received the floor lamp sans shade. Their email said, *"We're sorry to report that there has been a delay in the shipment of your items. We will ship the items as soon as they are available."*

And the emails never stopped. Final count: ten.

Since I didn't like staring at a shadeless lamp with a sixty-watt equivalent LED bulb glaring in my face, I picked up a shade at their mall store.

By month three, the lampshade arrived without much fanfare. Back to the store it must go.

"Do you have the receipt?" asked the store assistant, Zandra, as it prominently stated in bold font on her nametag. Her fussy, short bob and lacey eyelet collar perfectly suited her uptight attitude.

"It should be in the unopened box, right?" I said, lifting a single eyebrow.

It's standard Pottery Barn One-O-One.

"Definitely," said Zandra.

She ripped off the packing tape and stared. No receipt.

"When did you receive this?" she asked.

Come on, lady. It says right on the outside of the box. Read much?

After a few hundred more clicks on her terminal, she said, "Did you try to return it last month online?"

"How could I return something online when I just received it yesterday?"

Hey, what's with the twenty questions? Give. Me. My. Money.

"I'll get the store manager."

Seriously, just hand over the money and no one gets hurt.

The store manager proceeded to ask me all the same questions.

"Okay," she said, looking over the top of my head to see the next customer. "We can give you store credit."

"I don't want store credit. I still have some from another return. I would like it back on my credit card or cash."

"Since you ordered this online, I'll have to check with headquarters."

Is there anyone else I need to talk to?!?!?!

She proceeded to whisper into the phone and flagged over the original store assistant.

"We can offer you store credit," they said in unison.

"As I explained earlier, I do not want store credit. Can you put it back on my card?"

"Is this the card you used?" she said, pointing with rounded pink manicured nails at my order on the screen.

"Nope. It was stolen, and I got another card."

"How about a gift card?"

How about I flatten your tires?

"Fine."

I grabbed my gift card and headed out the door. On my way, I spied a blue brocaded pillow that would coordinate with my new sofa.

"Excuse me. Does this pillow come in a smaller size?"

"Don't know," the sales associate said with a glassy stare. "Check online."

And I suppose I should use this gift card?

SHENANIGANS

I'd like to be able to say that I've outgrown my juvenile fascination with shenanigans, but I'd be lying. Until my mug ends up on a post office wanted poster, I'm going to continue to cause mischief. That's how I roll.

Growing up in the '70s, my fascination with *Charlie's Angels* rivaled none other. The Angels' puffy hair, perfectly applied makeup, and edgy outfits transfixed me each Thursday night at 7:00 PM.

"Mom, we've got to go," I whined, staring at my grandparents' apartment walls, never failing to be amazed that so much clutter could fit in such little space. "*Charlie's Angels* is starting."

My angels are on in ten minutes. I need my fix.

"All right already. Stop pestering me," she said, with a heavy sigh. "We're leaving in a few."

Then a few minutes turned into five. Then eight.

"Come on," I said, pacing and darting a peek at my grandmother's vintage grinning Kit-Cat clock with wagging tail and rolling eyes. "We'll just barely get home by the opening credits."

How could she not understand that my life depended on this show?

Tick, tick, tick. The wall clock's black tail wagged back and forth and counted down the minutes at a hypnotic pace.

That's it!

"See ya later Grandma," I said as I breezily kissed her on the cheek and dragged my mother by the wrist out the door.

We'll just make it if the lights are all green, I thought.

From the passenger seat, I said, "Push the pedal to the metal, Mom. We can't miss this episode. Charlie needs the girls to catch a bank robber tonight."

She thrust the gearshift into drive and burned rubber out the asphalt parking lot.

Maybe it wasn't too late.

At the stop sign, she hit the gas and sped around the corner, cars honking in her wake. As we weaved through traffic, I was as nervous as an earthworm on hot concrete.

We're going to make it!

The glare of flashing red lights bounced off the rearview mirror, directing us to pull over.

"Ma'am, do you realize you were speeding?" said the officer as he sauntered up to the window.

Step it up. Got things to do!!

"My daughter needs to get home in time to watch *Charlie's Angels*," my mother said with a hopeful ring to her voice.

That's my girl.

Nonetheless, Mom received a ticket, but more importantly, I missed the opening to my show. On that day, I realized my shenanigans had consequences for others. But I still couldn't stop fooling around.

During college, my mischief-making led me to

believe that it would be easy peasy to conjure up a fake ID and sneak into the late night hot spots in downtown St. Louis. Armed with a roll of clear tape, scissors, and a newspaper, my minions and I fashioned fake ID's over our real ID's.

At the local dive bar, we boldly shouldered our way to the front of the line. The bouncer snatched the ID from my clammy outstretched hand, stapled it to the outdoor wall, and yelled "Next." My friends in line behind me scattered. We ended up at White Castle for late night fun instead. Not exactly the hot spot we imagined.

As an adult, my shenanigans continued.

In yoga class, I made fast friends with Louise, an English expat who moved to California after her husband was offered a job in Silicon Valley. As we put away our yoga props, she said, "I'm trying to help my daughter with decorations for her wedding. Any idea where I can find pampas grass?"

You've come to the right place.

Her daughter's wedding was one month away. As a tribute to her grandmother, she dreamed of decorating the event's archway with pampas grass, ornamental grasses that bloomed in mid-summer with big, fluffy white plumes. Fortunately for her, it grew in surplus in my neighborhood.

"Follow me. We'll scour my neighborhood. I even think I have some growing at my house."

"I need at least thirty stalks," she said eyeing my backyard.

"Let's go for a drive. I've spied some more over the hill. Bring your cutters."

"Won't that be stealing?"

"Nah, it's on common property between the homes.

Don't worry."

Truth be told, I had no idea about the rules in my community.

Like Lucy and Ethel, we took a road trip up and down my "hood" in search of the reedy plant.

"Over there," I said, pointing across the street. One jumbo bush made an excellent specimen, prime for the picking. Its long plumes stretched out from the backyard fence and into common property.

"Grab your clippers. Cut it down. I'll wait in the car in case someone stops."

"Are you sure this is okay? Remember, I just have a green card. I don't want to be deported."

"Don't worry. If we get stopped by the police, I'll just drive off and get you later."

"What?"

"I'm joking. But if I honk the horn, wrap it up."

I eyeballed from the driver's seat as Louise snipped away with clippers. Some of the fronds reached over eight feet tall. She turned into a flurry of prickly fluff with bloody cuts all over her arms.

After snipping her fill, she hustled back to the car and piled the booty into the trunk.

Breathless she asked, "Have you always been a hooligan?"

Hmmm, let me think for a second...yes.

KEEP YOUR HANDS TO YOURSELF

A strange woman fondled my breasts, trapped me in an awkward position, and called me cruel names. For a while, I tolerated her poor treatment.

I was getting a breast exam.

If you're like me, you postpone getting an annual mammogram for as long as possible. It hurts. But that little voice in your head keeps nagging, "Get it over with. It won't be so bad this time."

Hogwash.

On the day of my annual mammogram, I entered Mercy Healthcare, my stomach as knotted as Courtney Love's hair. A young assistant, with a pixie cut and cotton scrubs, sporting pink, blue, and white butterflies and hearts, carried a clipboard and led me into the changing area.

"Strip to the waist," she said with a wide smile. "Put on this gown. Wait for the technician."

Moments later, a stocky lady with mousey brown hair, smelling like she just finished a Taco Bell beef burrito for lunch, strutted into the room and yelled, "Next."

That's me.

I shadowed her to the exam area and gawked at the massive mammogram machine. Like a robot in *WALL-E*, a giant white box dominated the room with blue dangling tubes and hoses. Computers with jumbo screens circled the area.

Then I made a rookie mistake.

"Welcome to the torture chamber," I said in a loud voice. Crabby Patty hesitated, turned toward me, and stared me down with beady brown eyes.

"Oh, you're one of those?" she said, hands on her wide hips. "Are you going to complain the whole time? Would you rather get cancer?"

Gee, that's a leap. Lighten up, Francis.

"You must have a low tolerance for pain," she said with a snap of her head.

That's it, woman. One more word and I'm gonna let it rip.

But I decided to wait until after my mammogram before saying a word. I worried the machine might "accidentally" break in the middle and leave me trapped in its pneumatic grip.

Woman squeezed to death by The Machine.

After she pulled my gown aside, leaving me exposed and shivering, she pressed my body against the mammogram machine with her hands, forcing my right breast on a flat support plate.

She shoved my head to the right. "Now push your butt out," she demanded. "Bend your right knee. Suck in your stomach. Hold your breath."

Is that all? Want me to sing the Star-Spangled Banner? Recite the alphabet backward?

She proceeded to manhandle my breasts like a butcher with a side of beef. She squeezed, prodded,

and groped me into submission.
What? No small talk first?
"Now don't move," she said as she walked to the control panel.
Where would I go? If I fall, I am going to have to buy some new bras.
She pushed a button to compress my breast with a parallel plate called a paddle.
The machine flattened my breast like a Swedish pancake. Due to the awkward position, I shifted my weight to the other leg.
"This will go faster if you cooperate," she hissed in my ear.
Click.
An x-ray was taken. Then the whole process was repeated,
When it finally ended, she tossed me my flimsy gown and with a smirk said, "See how easy that was? Aren't you embarrassed you complained?"
I warned you.
"Lady, for your information, I have an unusually high tolerance for pain," I said clenching my teeth. "I delivered two babies, ten pounds each, same as a pigmy hippopotamus. One without pain medication."
Take that.
"And I've had shoulder surgery, my gallbladder removed, and get my eyebrows waxed every two months."
Now, who's the baby?
I snatched my things and scooted out. And yes, I say it still hurts. Enough to skip a mammogram? Of course not.
This public service announcement brought to you in

conjunction with breast cancer awareness month. Like their slogan says, "Big or Small, Let's Save Them All."

WAYS TO DIE IN CANADA

I never imagined a trip to Canada would prove to be hazardous to my health. Let me explain.

As my family of four planned our summer vacation, we considered going on an extreme vacation, like swimming with the sharks in the Bahamas or zip-lining over Niagara Falls. We wanted something that was really cutting edge, something extreme. However, we realized that we're too lazy, so we picked Canada. The exact opposite of extreme.

We could not have been more misinformed.

Our excursion started with a train ride on the Rocky Mountaineer from Vancouver to Jasper. For two days, we were treated to spectacular wildlife and scenery like black bears, elk, and Athabasca Falls. Each day, we rode for eight nonstop hours, punctuated by breakfast, lunch, and an endless stream of snacks and drinks.

A two-hour break between breakfast and lunch, ludicrous!

After breakfast on the first day, our tour guide/server/bartender shared common interest stories about the view beyond our train windows. At this point, it became apparent that Canada was extremely dangerous.

Jeremy, our guide, kept a running monologue of

tragic accidents along the way. Within the first hour, he said, "Look out the window to the right. That's the site of a tragic mudslide, wiped out the whole town. Bodies still buried beneath the mud."

After ten minutes he announced, "Up ahead is the location of the Hinton Train Collision of 1986, the most lethal in Canada. Twenty-three people killed and ninety-five others sustained injuries, between a Canadian National Railway freight train and a VIA Rail Canada passenger train, due to the use of a "dead man's pedal." We learned that the dead man's pedal was a heavy weight which a locomotive engineer used in case he fell asleep.

What?!? You can drive a train while sleeping?

For the next fifty miles, he continued to ramble on about deadly explosions, forest fires, elk attacks, hypothermia, and death by heavy machinery. Body count totaled 2,989. And that was just last year. This was feeling like a PBS travelogue, *Rick Steves' Ways to Die in Canada*.

To unwind from the tragic news, we continue to feast. Like Kobe beef, we were fattened up with nonstop meals and snacks, plus an unlimited supply of beer and spirits.

"Would you like another drink?" our host asked.

"Of course," we responded.

As we were nearly lulled to sleep by the overconsumption of carbs and alcohol, Jeremy continued to talk.

In Jasper, we departed the train and transferred to a shuttle bus with fifty other passengers. At our first stop, Linda, the bus driver and tour guide, issued the first of many bear warnings.

"If you decide to get off and wander, bring a can of

bear spray," she said in an unassuming manner, popping her gum and smiling. "It's a lot like pepper spray but only use if you get within three meters of a bear. Spray into the eyes and nose."

What's this? If I get within three meters of a bear, I'm going to spray it into my own eyes to avoid watching myself be mauled.

Needless to say, most passengers stayed on the bus. As we proceeded to the next stop, she pointed out other local disasters. "Look out to your left. That's the site of the Frank Slide, ninety million tons of limestone rock slid down within 100 seconds. The whole town was wiped out, including the Canadian Pacific Railway line and the coal mine. Most residents remain buried in the rubble."

Holy shit!

The last part of our Canadian adventure included a twelve-minute Rocky Mountain helicopter ride over glaciers, mountain vistas, lakes, and waterfalls. Before departing, we anticipated an extensive precautionary safety check.

However, Eric, a pimply-faced, bored attendant, said in a blasé manner, "Hey folks. Take a number from the peg board and wait your turn."

Our family boarded the helicopter, my daughter in front and the rest of us in the second row. Jonathan, our overqualified ex-military pilot, introduced himself through the headsets and away we went. About midway through our flight, we heard him say, "Oops." This has to be bad, I thought. Then he leaned over and shut the passenger door. It had popped open.

We were so happy to be back on the ground, we left without even asking for a free photo.

In hindsight, we should have taken our chances in the Bahamas with the sharks. In my defense, all the Canadian travel brochures looked so melancholy.

MICK JAGGER KEEPS ME UP AT NIGHT

"Why'd you send me email at midnight with the link, *1,000 Ways to Clean Lint Out of the Dryer?*" said my best friend, Jackie. I could feel her eyebrows squish together through the phone line.

"Can we talk?" I said as I adjusted my eyeglasses and slumped into the nearest reclining chair. "It was a long night,"

You asked for it, babe.

"I couldn't get a wink of sleep," I said forcing a laugh. After getting only a few hours of restful sleep at night. I was exhausted every day.

"Nothing went right over the weekend. Lost car keys. Broken garage door. Fight with husband. Argument over homework with the kids," I complained. "I just wanted to snuggle in bed and forget about the day, catch some serious shut-eye. But no, no, no."

"I know how you feel," she said with a sigh. "Some days it's impossible to clear your mind and go back to bed."

My night unraveled as fast as a ball of yarn rolling

down the stairs. Our mattress was as lumpy as steel-cut oatmeal. I felt hot, like I was going to suffocate. And what the hell was wrong with the alarm clock? Tick, tick, tock. Like a metronome, over and over. Tick, tick, tock. And the infuriating nightlight. As bright as a lighthouse beacon. How come I didn't notice that before? Who can fall asleep with all this commotion?

My mind wouldn't turn off. Did I leave the oven on? What time is my dentist appointment? Did the kids remember to pack their lunch? I glared at my hubby as he snored next to me. That man has actually slept through an earthquake and a fire alarm. On the same night. What kind of person can sack out like that? He must be a psychopath.

Worst yet, that Adam Levine song stuck in my head, repeating over and over… "You want the moves like Jagger, / I've got the moves like Jagger, / I've got the movesssssss…like Jagger.

What's that bump on my face? Do I have a tumor? Where did I put my eyeglasses? What if there's an earthquake and I need to get out?

"I don't need to control you, / Look into my eyes and I'll own you…"

That song played itself over and over my head.

Argh! Make it stop!

For an hour I contemplated the ceiling, praying for slumber. I counted sheep. Then I counted backward. Finally, I popped out of bed to surf the Internet in the office.

You win Jagger!

I pressed the button on the back of the Mac and booted up. Hmmm. Hmmm. Hmmmm. Music to my ears. Maybe I could finally get Adam Levine out of my brain.

Fingers perched on top the keys, I held my breath in anticipation. Wait a minute. What's this? I stared in a trance at a clip of *Keeping Up with the Kardashians*. Another one pregnant? A friendship tested? Missing cell phone? Oh, my. Within moments, I felt consumed by the problems of the rich and famous. Click, click.

Or what about that potty-mouth kid that gets his leg cast sawed off? I couldn't stop listening to him throw curse words. I replayed the video in an endless loop.

Oh my god, is that Richard Simmons in a gold leotard, Sweatin' to the Oldies? He's still alive? Click, click.

Two hours, and 1,897 clicks later, my head drooped over the keyboard. For a brief moment, I snapped awake and crawled back under the covers.

"I've got the moves like Jagger, / I've got the moves like Jagger…"

I'll take a nap on the sofa in the afternoon after the kids get home from school. It's quieter.

YOU'LL THANK ME LATER

I admit it. When it comes to remodeling, some things are better left to the experts. I've made bad decisions in the past. Enlisting my son's help to change the kitchen lighting may have been one of them. But he seemed so competent. He claimed he could do it since we spent hours watching HGTV. In his defense, it was my fault for asking in the first place. After all, second grade's entirely too young to operate an electric drill.

It all started with a sink faucet. For years, I battled Mr. Spray. If you didn't hold the handle just right, his water splattered the backsplash, windowsill, and my face. When a plumber suggested it was time for an upgrade, I said, "Show me the spigot." Lucky for me, he conveniently had a new pull-down, stainless steel faucet in his truck and time to install it.

Bada bing bada boom.

Then the new faucet got me thinking.

"Honey, our kitchen's looking sad and outdated," I said to my husband as he devoured the last piece of lasagna. "What do you think about a remodel?"

"Could you get it done when I'm out of town?"

"No problem," I said.

We agreed it would be my project and he wouldn't interfere. Due to his travel plans, he'd be too occupied to bother.

"What about a budget?" he asked.

Laura Spendthrift, our decorator, helped us determine a rough estimate for cabinets, lighting, curtains, and tile for the backsplash. With a flash of her pearly whites and trendy blond hair, she said, "That's it. This will be easy."

"Sounds fair," Mike said reviewing her spreadsheet.

"Don't worry," she said as she tilted her head back and shook Mike's hand. "We've covered it all. Shouldn't be any surprises."

Her stacked charm bracelets jangled as she bolted out the front door. Mike gave me the side eye and said, "I trust you'll stay within this figure?"

"Of course."

On Monday, she dispatched John Workman from Dynamite Construction to evaluate the scope of work.

"Laura told me you wanted to repaint your old cabinet doors and drawers," said John as he shuffled into the room and circled around the kitchen island. "I'll do a paint test and let you know in a few days if it's possible."

Originally, I wanted to save money by adding a new coat of paint to the old stuff, a simple and cheap alternative to replacement.

Easy peasy lemon squeezy.

But when John returned he said, "No good. Won't hold the paint. The previous owners brush painted the doors with latex. If you paint over this, it will crack and slide off."

"Dang," I said.

"I think you should invest in brand new doors. I'll adjust the quote. You'll thank me later."

Additions and changes were adding up as fast as an AP honors math student using a scientific calculator. As he gazed around the kitchen, John had more to say.

"Think it would look nicer if you added more crown molding."

"How much will that cost?" I asked.

"Not much," he said as he took notes on his iPhone. "You'll thank me later."

He continued to strut around my kitchen with suggestions. "I can turn that wasted space under the stove top into a pull-out drawer."

A regular Harry Houdini.

"Um…how much will that cost?"

"I'll send you the adjusted figures in a few days. Don't worry about it now. You'll thank me later.

"You keep saying that. I'm getting the impression you'd prefer if I blew up the whole kitchen and started over."

He laughed and turned away. Over his shoulder, he said, "Don't worry. It'll turn out fine."

After four weeks, he had replaced the backsplash, cabinet doors, and drawers, added halogen lighting, dishwasher, curtains, baked a cake, and blew me a kiss.

I stood back to suck it all in.

"Here's the final bill, payable in the next seven days," John said with a wink as he slapped it down on the counter.

Plop.

After work, my husband gazed around the room. "Everything looks fabulous," he said giving me the thumbs-up. "How'd you do it all and stay in the budget?"

"Little over budget," I said as I cleared my throat. "You'll thank me later."

ACKNOWLEDGEMENTS

Thanks to all my family and friends for allowing me to make their private lives public. I'd like to thank my husband, Mike, who supports me in my writing endeavors and never gets mad when he's part of my jokes. He's handsome too. I'd like to thank my children, Ashley and Brock, who allow me to write about their antics despite the fact that they are both over eighteen and should have demanded to sign a permission waiver in order to be published in this book. Since I am sure they will never read this page, it's too late.

I'd like to thank my parents who allow me to express myself and still consider me the best kid in the world. Thanks for letting me out of punishments when I was young just because I made you laugh.

To Ed Miracle, outstanding writer and friend. Thanks for your suggestions.

Other thanks go out to Luminare Press, especially my gifted publisher, Patricia Marshall, and editor, Kim Harper-Kennedy. Yes, the process is easier the second time around. Thanks to Claire Flint Last, graphic designer. You were right. Yellow is way better than pink.

Big thanks go out to Regina Stoops for letting me do stand-up with her at Tommy T's Comedy Club for the first time. That moment changed everything.

Special gratitude goes to Camille DeFer Thompson, my dear friend, fabulous humor writer, and critique partner. Thanks for dropping everything to help me when I panic. In return, I will continue to keep all your secrets.

Thank you also to Erma Bombeck Writers' Workshop, especially Gina Valley, Vikki Claflin, Elaine Ambrose, Teri Rizvi, Jim Hands, Leighann Lord, Wendy Liebman, Linda Wolff, Anne Paris, Tracy Beckerman, Linda Roy, Lisa Packer, Marcia Kester Doyle, Dorothy Rosby, Donna Beckman Tagliaferri, Stephanie Mark Lewis, and Risa Nye. You are my people.

ABOUT STACEY

STACEY GUSTAFSON is the bestselling author of *Are You Kidding Me? My Life with an Extremely Loud Family, Bathroom Calamities, and Crazy Relatives*, ranked #1 Amazon in Parenting & Family Humor and Motherhood. She's also an inspirational speaker, blogger, and comedian. Her short stories have appeared in *Chicken Soup for the Soul* and other in print and online publications. Her awards include Erma Bombeck Humor Writer of the Month.

She lives in Pleasanton, California with her college sweetheart, Mike, and a white furball named Stanley who loves peanut butter treats. Visit Stacey at StaceyGustafson.com and Twitter @RUKiddingStacey.

Thanks for laughing along with me!

If you enjoyed *Are You Still Kidding Me?*, please consider telling your friends or posting a quick review on Amazon. It's like giving an author a hug.

Thanks again!

Made in the USA
San Bernardino, CA
23 February 2019